BLOCK PRINTING
ON TEXTILES

BLOCK PRINTING

ON TEXTILES

A Complete Guide

JANET ERICKSON

A WATSON-GUPTILL PUBLICATION

1961

To Eric

TABLE OF CONTENTS

PREFACE

THIS IS AN UNUSUAL BOOK by an unusual author. For, more than anyone else in America today, Janet Doub Erickson has lifted a craft that had become dull, dead, and dated to a position where we can see its challenging possibilities in the creative renaissance we are now experiencing. Literally with her bare feet, she has brought to *Block Printing on Textiles* a new dynamic and artistic quality that we had come to believe did not exist in an area dominated by listless checkerboard stereotypes and hackneyed commercial offerings. She is a designer-craftsman in the finest sense of the word. Her designs are composed with the spontaneity and vitality of the contemporary artist. Her knowledge of technical processes has been enriched through a long experience in practical production for clients, including a period as partner in the Block House in Boston, enabling her to share with the reader many of her own discoveries in techniques.

Her work has been exhibited widely, and she has been active in craftsmen's organizations in Massachusetts and New York. Her work was awarded first prize in the textile division of the 1954 Young Americans exhibition, sponsored by the American Craftsmen's Council. Unlike some craftsmen distinguished for their own production, Janet Erickson is an excellent teacher who unselfishly shares her own findings with others and inspires her students to creative work. Students from many areas of the United States studied with her at the summer crafts workshops sponsored by the State of Connecticut. Art students at the State College of Education at Buffalo were inspired by her teaching and her enthusiasm for the medium. A graduate of the Massachusetts School of Art, she brings to this medium the orientation of the artist-designer. Recently she made a study of textiles in Mexico under a Tiffany fellowship grant.

When the author tells you that block printing is fun, she refers to the deeper sense of satisfaction that comes from creating one's own, rather than the superficial use of that word in current how-to-do-it books. When she tells you that it is easy, she refers to the ease with which one may fall in love with the craft, and "love's labor's easy." A good book is like a good teacher, and this is one of them. It will be received with enthusiasm by the serious designer-craftsman and any who are looking for a dynamic, creative approach to an interesting art. It will serve as a sorely needed reference and textbook for classes in art, industrial arts, home economics, and in other areas of design.

Dr. Kenneth Winebrenner, *Editor*
School Arts Magazine

INTRODUCTION

A WOMAN who had never done any block printing telephoned me one day, before coming to class in a workshop that I was directing, to ask if ten yards of fabric would be too much to bring to the first class meeting. She planned to get her living room draperies out of the way during the first session.

While applauding the spirit of this ambitious approach, I had to point out that it is best to limit one's first effort in block printing to a small project that can be completed quickly, providing a background of experience in all the techniques, from planning and cutting a block through printing and color setting. Having once completed this cycle, even a neophyte can begin to enjoy the excitement of creative inventiveness as he experiments with variations on his basic ideas, and if the first experimental project is a small one, scraps of fabric requiring no investment can be used.

This book is designed to answer practically every question that could conceivably come up about block printing. The chapters are arranged consecutively from a description of the equipment needed through special projects requiring advanced techniques.

It takes much longer to read about block printing than it does to do it. The beginner who wishes to rush through his first project can leave much of this material for later digestion. Once the necessary equipment is assembled, anyone can cut, mount, and print a simple block in less than an hour.

Block printing is a very ancient craft. The first *printed* books were made in the Orient in the ninth century, cut and impressed from wood blocks in ink on paper. The woodcut made its appearance in Europe in the fifteenth century, printed on paper — but there exist examples of block printing on *cloth* by the Egyptian Copts several hundred years earlier.

Those who have tried it know that block printing is fun. They have found great satisfaction in making something that expressed their own sense of beauty and order. Block printing is also an inexpensive and uncomplicated craft. Its technical simplicity allows a tremendous range of personal expression, while at the same time it can produce a really useful and practical result.

Once you have mastered the basic techniques, you will be able to hand-block draperies suitable for a period drawing room or for an informal bedroom. You can print gay café curtains for a kitchen with tablecloth, napkins, and apron to match, or you might brighten a child's room with a whimsical wall hanging. Hand-blocked prints launder beautifully and are practical for couch covers, slip covers, and bed spreads. Table linens printed in your original designs make elegant gifts, and you can add to their attractiveness by wrapping them in hand-blocked paper. You can also print cards and even wallpaper.

Nothing is more fun to wear than a colorful design which you have printed yourself. Perhaps your fancy will be attracted to decorating a skirt or a shirt. You can also print handsome bathing suits, beach jackets, vests, scarves, stoles, neckties, shorts — in fact, anything that will take a printed impression. You can print on garments which are ready-made, or, if you are a clever seamstress, you might even try such elaborate projects as ball gowns and evening dresses. But, whether the article is large or small, ready-made or sewn by hand, it will have the unique quality that your design and your craftsmanship have given it.

In this book I have outlined all the successful block printing techniques that I know. You can choose the one that you will enjoy most and that suits your circumstances best. There is no one right way to print; so you can make up your own set of rules as you gain experience — another reason block printing is so fascinating.

BLOCK PRINTING ON TEXTILES

PART

1 *Assembling a Block Printing Kit*

YOU CAN BLOCK PRINT WITH ALMOST ANYTHING. For instance, a few years ago a young Swiss who sailed a small boat single-handed around the world wrote that he amused himself in mid-ocean by block printing. Perhaps, rather than cutting designs in linoleum, he may have inked the backbone of a fish and printed with that, with the fish itself, or with a textured piece of wood or rope.

Exciting prints have been made by rolling an automobile tire across a fabric and also by printing the inked needles of a branch from a pine tree. By exerting varying degrees of ingenuity, elbow grease, and imagination you can block print with such different materials as rubber tile, plastic screening, plasticene, soft pine blocks, cork flooring, art gum erasers, styrofoam, and sponges.

LINOLEUM

Although you can block print with practically anything under the sun, most craftsmen prefer linoleum. Not all linoleum, however, is equally suitable for block printing. Ideally, it should be soft enough to cut easily with simple gouge tools, hold its shape well, and stand up under literally miles of printing. Several linoleums are excellent and their costs range from ten cents to several dollars a yard. But avoid mounted linoleum blocks with a white surface. They are made from hard, brittle linoleum and are almost impossible to cut. The heavy wood backing makes them clumsy to handle when printing. They discourage rather than aid beginning block printers.

An excellent linoleum for block printing is marketed as "countertop" or "desk-top." This thin, dark gray linoleum costs about four dollars a square yard and is usually sold by wholesale dealers only. The linoleum dealer in your town or city will generally be obliging enough to find the local source if you agree to buy a yard or two at a time to make it worth his while.

Much less expensive, and just about as satisfactory, is the type of linoleum called "border-strip," which can be bought in almost any linoleum store. It comes in long rolls, nine or twelve inches wide, and it costs from ten to twenty-five cents a linear yard. For small blocks or for long narrow ones it is fine. You can glue several sections onto your backing to form a large piece if you need a big square block. The joints will be invisible if you undercut each edge a bit and then squeeze the joints as you join the glued surfaces.

GOUGES

You need gouges to cut a design in the linoleum. Some craftsmen have made their own gouges by sharpening a three-inch length

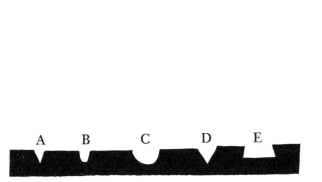

A deep V

B deep U

C shallow, wide U (background tool)

D razor blade

E razor blade (for very sharp edge, good for clean lettering)

16

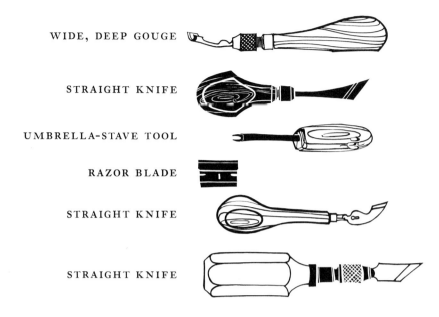

WIDE, DEEP GOUGE

STRAIGHT KNIFE

UMBRELLA-STAVE TOOL

RAZOR BLADE

STRAIGHT KNIFE

STRAIGHT KNIFE

of steel umbrella stave and setting it in a wooden handle. However, there are a number of inexpensive, domestically made and some imported sets of gouges that are excellent. When buying, choose one gouge with a deep V-point, another with an equally deep U-shape, and a wider, flatter U-shaped gouge for cutting out background areas quickly. If you buy a set of gouges that are meant to be used interchangeably in a chuck-type handle, it is a good idea to buy separate handles for each gouge. It will save you the inconvenience of having to shift points when you want a different width of line. You can buy an excellent set of gouges for as little as one dollar.

A small oilstone or carborundum stone should be in your kit so that you can keep the edges of your cutting tools sharp. The surface of the stone should be lubricated with a drop of oil and the cutting edge of the gouge rubbed quickly back and forth over it. Check the edge of the point on your thumbnail as you work on it to make sure you are sharpening, not dulling it.

INKS

Most art stores sell four ounce tubes of block printing inks which are economical if you want only a small amount of color, although some of these inks are not very brilliant, and a few of the reds have proved unreliable in use. Inks are either oil base or water base. Water base inks are useless for printing on fabric, since the ink is soluble in water. They are meant for printing on paper or for use in elementary schools or other situations when it is difficult to work with oils and turpentine.

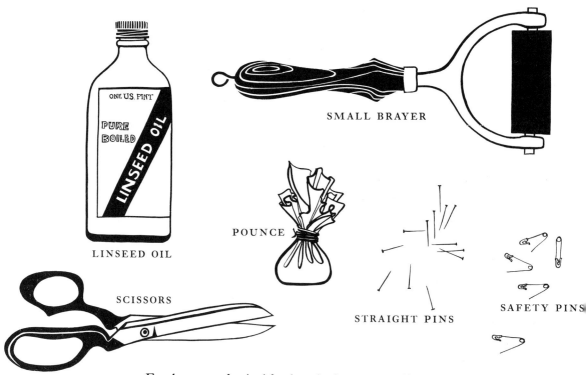

LINSEED OIL

SMALL BRAYER

POUNCE

SCISSORS

STRAIGHT PINS

SAFETY PINS

For best results in block printing on textiles, you will probably want to buy oil base printer's inks, which are packaged in eight-inch tubes and in cans in quantities from one-half pound up. These strong, brilliant, and sunfast colors are sold ready to use and can be stored indefinitely without deterioration. There are many brands of oil base printer's inks available. Be sure to specify "non-fugitive"

18

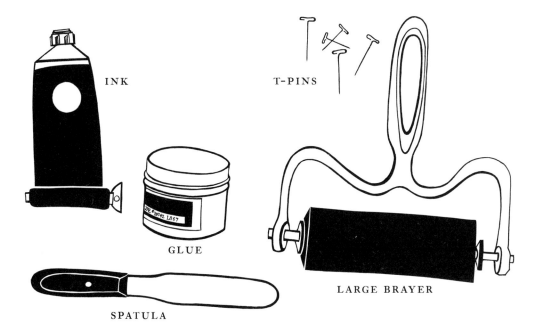

INK

T-PINS

GLUE

LARGE BRAYER

SPATULA

colors when ordering. These are the colors that will not fade. They are also intermixable. Red, yellow, and blue, plus black and white will mix to make almost any color. Some pigments weigh more than others, so the prices of colors vary.

There are two kinds of printer's white inks: opaque "cover white" and transparent mixing base. The covering power of transparent base has been reduced by the addition of a bulky colorless filler. It is much cheaper than cover white. A color mixed with it becomes semi-transparent. For instance, red mixed with base and printed on bright yellow will show as orange. To make a color stay true on a strong color background, mix it with cover white.

For some kinds of printing on paper, poster paints can be used with interesting results. Artists' oil paints generally have too little body to be used by themselves for block printing. However, they can be used successfully to *tint* block printing inks.

PALETTE AND PALETTE KNIVES

For spreading out and mixing your inks you need a palette. Any smooth, flat, non-absorbent surface will do. A sheet of glass makes a good palette. The edges should be ground down or taped to protect your hands and the brayer from cuts. Place a sheet of white paper under the glass to reflect light so that you will be able to see your colors clearly. A good size for a palette for most projects would be twenty inches square. Window glass can be used, but plate glass is better. You can get second-hand plate glass from a window display supplier or a glazier. A smooth metal plate, sheet of Masonite, or a slab of marble can also be used for a palette. Marble will stain, but it can be scrubbed clean again if the ink is not allowed to set too long.

A sheet of celluloid or shellacked cardboard or wood can substitute for more durable materials if you are in need of a makeshift palette. None of these is too successful as a permanent palette, however, since they curl and shred during prolonged use.

To manipulate the ink on the palette table you will need some spatulas. The short flexible knives used in oil painting are a bit too delicate for our purposes. Instead, buy sturdy spatulas from the kitchenware department of a dime store. The longer-bladed ones are best for handling the inks, but you will need a short one for cleaning out paint cans and other necessary chores. You will need at least two palette knives.

BRAYER

Still to be added to your equipment is a roller, more properly called a brayer. Your brayer must be smooth and true all the way around. It can be made of gelatine, plastic, or solid rubber, and it should be mounted in a sturdy wooden handle that allows it to rotate freely. It should not be too soft, nor too hard. A brayer made of gelatine must never be used with water-base inks because water will dissolve the gelatine.

Most designers use a gelatine "proof brayer," which you can

buy for about four dollars from a printer's supply house or through your local printer. Specify that you want it mounted in a handle. This brayer will be six inches long and one and one-half to two inches in diameter. It will last indefinitely in ordinary use. Used constantly, it will break down in about nine months. When it does, you can have the gelatine core recast for about two dollars and fifty cents. Also, smaller gelatine brayers are useful for inking small designs. A three-inch gelatine brayer is available, but it costs almost twice as much as the larger one because it is cut down from the six-inch size. A smaller brayer is useful for inking small, delicate designs.

Several companies make excellent plastic brayers. In appearance and texture they are identical to gelatine and apparently never wear out. They cost around ten dollars but prove a good investment. The price of plastic brayers should go down as more companies get into the market.

There are six-inch, three-inch, and two-inch soft, solid rubber brayers mounted in strong wooden handles. You can buy these by mail from several companies that advertise in art and craft magazines. The large size is slightly more expensive than the gelatine, but the smaller ones cost less.

The hard rubber rollers that are sold in art stores as block printing brayers are *not* adequate for block printing on fabric. Usually made with a thin layer of rubber over a wooden base, they are hard and uneven and deposit either too much or too little ink on the block. They cost slightly less than a gelatine brayer but are a total loss. It is impossible to make a good print using one of them. If you have one already, throw it away. Or better yet, plan an overall pattern and score the rubber heavily with a knife and use the brayer to roll interesting textural background onto your fabric.

You can ink a small block with a "pounce," which can be made by wrapping a rag around a wad of cotton waste or another rag. Flatten the bottom of the pounce by pounding it on a flat surface. To use it, dip it in the ink, bounce it several times on the palette to spread the ink evenly over the bottom, and dab it on the block.

BACKING BOARDS

The thin, soft linoleums are quite flexible. When a design is cut in a fairly large piece it becomes so floppy that it is difficult to handle and should be mounted on a stiff backing board. For most blocks meant to be printed on fabric, a piece of heavy cardboard provides sufficiently strong backing. The cardboard should be heavy enough not to bend easily.

The heavy gray cardboard called "pasted chipboard" is excellent for backing large blocks. This is the kind of cardboard used to back drawing, sketching, and tracing paper pads. You can buy single sheets from an art supply store or get it by the bundle from a paper dealer. It comes in several different weights and in twenty by thirty inch sheets. A bundle contains fifteen to thirty sheets, depending upon their weight and thickness, and will cost about four dollars.

Very large linoleum designs are best mounted on the fiber wallboard called Upsom Board. It can be cut with a mat knife or a strong, single-edge razor blade. You can buy it from a lumber yard or from a hardware store that sells construction supplies. It comes in four by eight foot sheets and costs about three dollars a sheet. You can usually have it cut into two or three pieces of manageable size where you buy it. A very large block could be mounted on a pressed wood board, Masonite, or plywood, but these materials are heavy and sometimes make the block awkward and difficult to place on the fabric when printing.

GLUES

You will need glue for mounting the linoleum on the backing board. There are several kinds available. Casein glues dry hard almost immediately, thus eliminating the need to set the glued block under pressure. Small blocks can be mounted using rubber cement, but remember that rubber cement dries and loses its adhesive quality after several months. Water-soluble liquid glues set hard and firm in four to six hours under pressure.

22

The cheapest glues are those you mix yourself. Horsehide and fish glues are sold in powder form in some hardware stores. Art supply stores sell rabbitskin glue in sheets. These glues are inexpensive but you must mix them yourself. This is simple to do, but a messy, smelly job. Ask for instructions where you buy them.

ADDITIONAL EQUIPMENT

You will also need boiled linseed oil to thin your inks and a solvent to clean blocks, brayers, and palette. The boiled linseed oil can be purchased from a hardware store. It sells for about sixty cents a pint. Kerosene is an effective and inexpensive solvent. You can usually find it at a hardware store or gasoline station, and it should cost about twenty cents a gallon, if you provide your own container. Turpentine is also a good solvent, but more expensive than kerosene. *Warning:* Remember that both of the latter materials are highly inflammable.

The mounted block is not ready to be printed until the backing board has been shellacked, although you may make trial prints before this finish is added. (You can use either white or orange shellac.)

Tools for measuring and cutting are needed. You should have a carpenter's square or a steel-edge ruler, a T-square and a triangle to measure with and to make accurate angles. To cut the linoleum and the backing you will need a sharp mat knife set in a sturdy handle, or you can use a single-edge razor blade. You will also need a pair of sharp scissors for cutting fabric, and a pair of heavy shears is useful for cutting linoleum and light backing.

A few additional items will complete your block printing kit. You should have a sturdy work table and an apron or smock. You will also need a box of T-pins. These are strong wire pins in the shape of a T, about two inches long, used by tailors and furriers. The T protects your finger when pushing the point of the pin into the bed. A ball of strong light twine, a couple of pencils, some tracing paper, a sponge, a small scrub brush, a length of clothesline, and a pile of newspapers and rags should complete your equipment.

PART

Ideas are all around you

2 *Preparing the Block*

PLANNING YOUR BLOCK

WHAT IS A TEXTILE DESIGN? A textile design is a design
that enriches the surface of a fabric. It need not have a "center of
interest," or depth, or up and down, or recognizable pictorial elements. In fact it is generally best if it has none of these things. It
must, however, have a quality of unmonotonous richness that could
be visualized as continuing for miles without tiring your eyes.

Generally speaking, the purpose for which the fabric is to be
used is always the most important factor in planning how to develop the design. A drapery fabric can have a larger, bolder pattern
than a dress fabric. A necktie pattern will be a different type from a
design planned to be printed on table linen. A fabric that will be
draped must be considered as it falls into folds. This draping will
destroy, or at least distort, any naturalistic elements in the design.
This does not mean that you should use only abstract elements in
your design, but you must be aware that the design will not look
the same draped as it did when laid out flat.

Designing is fun, and designing a textile pattern is a lot easier

Boldly stylized flower for placemat

Linoleum block using historical material

*Fine-scale drapery design
inspired by spider webs*

Stylized leaves for drapery

26

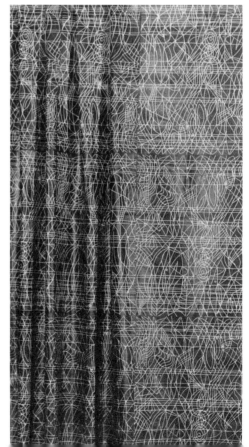

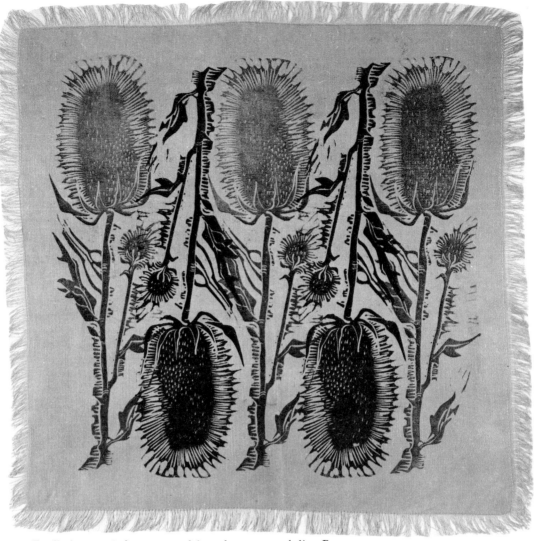

Realistic use of thorny teasel for placemat — Arline Bauer

than you might think. Ideas for designs are all around you. You might be inspired by the thread-like construction of a spiderweb or a simple form of plant life magnified in a microscope, by the shape of a snow crystal or even the molecular structure of the atom. Your designing imagination might be stimulated by a book like the *Index of American Design* or by some of the beautifully illustrated books on the folk arts of other countries.

Sometimes it helps if you keep a folder into which you can slip notes of your design ideas and clippings that seem to have possibilities. Cultivate an awareness of the design of fabrics you see in daily

Overlapping, spontaneous design
not requiring preliminary sketches — Agnes Fromer

use. Pick one you like and analyze why you like it. *Does it balance formally or freely? Does it use texture effectively to enhance the design? Is the color bold and definite or subtle and quiet? Is the design appropriate for the spot where it is used? Would it be useful other places as well? Do the spaces where the design is not (the negative spaces) form interesting shapes?*

If you like working with abstract shapes, a collection of scraps of colored paper is useful. You can snip out the shapes you are thinking of using and try various arrangements of them to help you in deciding exactly how to make your blocks. Sometimes, too, the accidental shapes of the scraps themselves will give you new ideas.

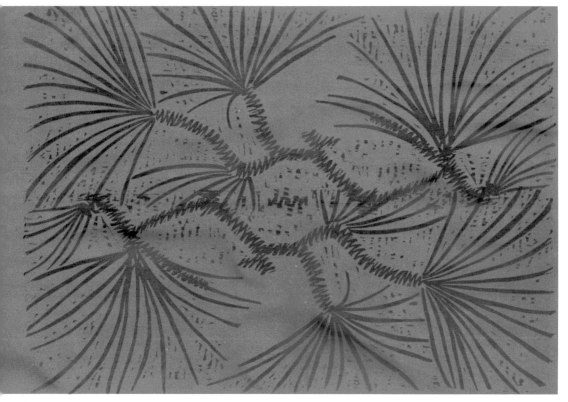

Silk scarf showing effective use of tropical plants — Stell and Shevis

When you have settled on the idea for your design you must consider how it can be developed and adapted to best fit your purposes. *Should you use mostly lines or solid areas? You might use both. You can make a positive image or a negative one, or combine these effects. The motif can be stretched out, compressed, or distorted to fit a special shape, such as the corner of a scarf. Many things you may want to print will have corners. You cannot ignore them. They must be taken into account when planning the design.*

A design that is very angular can be enriched with texture. Consider the texture of the fabric you are printing as well as the different textural effects you can cut into the block itself. A very simple design of solid areas can be enriched by printing it on linen with a rough heavy weave. A design of fine web-like lines will look even more delicate printed on fragile silk.

A realistic design is successfully adapted to the square shape of a table cloth by printing one L-shaped block four times

30

A precise design worked out with the aid of preliminary sketches

Some people like to begin without preliminary sketches, cutting directly into the linoleum with the gouges. Seeing the various kinds of lines and shapes made by the cutting tools helps them to decide what effects should be most prominent in the finished design. Others prefer a more careful approach. They will work out a sketch in detail on paper before transferring it to the linoleum to be cut. The method you use will depend partly upon the type of person you are and partly on the effect you want your design to have. A neat, precise design must be thoughtfully worked out and the blocks carefully made. A spontaneous design that uses color and textural effects in a free, loose way cannot be achieved by the same method.

1. *marking off a section of linoleum*

2. *scoring the marked lines*

3. *bending the linoleum along the scored lines*

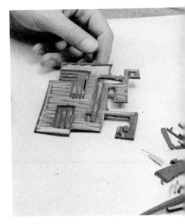

7. *gouging out the negative areas*

8. *cutting out large unwanted areas with scissors*

9. *the design ready for mounting*

13. *filling in outline with thin coat of glue*

14. *glueing back of design*

15. *matching the glued surfaces for accurate mounting*

32

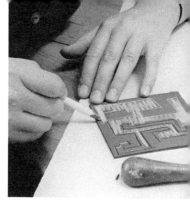

4. *strengthening the transferred design with white pencil*

5. *outlining the design area with a narrow gouge*

6. *whiting out the areas to avoid in cutting*

. *measuring and marking a section of backing board*

11. *cutting the backing board*

12. *outlining a guide for applying glue*

TRANSFERRING THE DESIGN TO LINOLEUM

If you have drawn your design on paper, measure the size of your design, place the linoleum face down on a smooth work table, and mark off a section of linoleum into which your design would fit. A T-square and a right angle triangle will help you to make accurate angles and correct measurements. Or, you could use a carpenter's square.

Using a steel-edge ruler as a guide, score the linoleum with a single-edge razor blade or a sharp knife along the lines that you have marked off. The linoleum should crack and part when you bend it back along the scored lines. If the cut has not been deep enough to separate the linoleum, run the knife along the cut again. Do not tear

33

or twist the linoleum because this will make a ragged edge that will have to be re-cut. Trim off with scissors any loose threads hanging from the backing.

Coat the back of the design with pastel or chalk, making a carbon of it. Place it, chalk side down, on the block and trace over the lines of your design with a sharp, fairly hard pencil. Check occasionally, as you are tracing, to see if your lines are transferring. As these chalk lines will brush off the surface of the linoleum rather easily, they should be strengthened directly on the block with a white pencil before you begin cutting.

Remember that printing with the block reverses your design. What is at the left side of the block, as you look at it, will be at the right side in the printed impression made from the block. This reversal does not usually become important unless lettering is incorporated into the design.

It is a simple matter to make a block that will give you an unreversed impression. Work out the design on tracing paper as you want it finally to appear. Then, turn the paper over. Bring the design through to the back of this paper. It will then be reversed. Now chalk the *front* side of the paper. Place this side against the block, transferring it, reversed, to the block.

Egypto-Arabic carved wooden block
Courtesy of The Metropolitan Museum of Art
Gift of V. Everit Macy, 1930

English 18th century wood block
Courtesy of The Metropolitan Museum of Art
Gift of C. P. and J. Baker, 1927

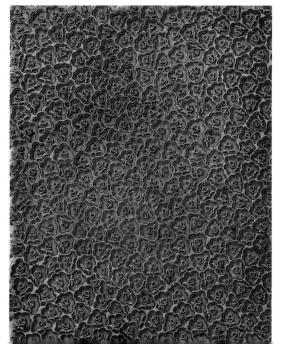

Pottery stamps from Equador   Melanesian incised bamboo
Courtesy of the American Museum of Natural History

CUTTING THE BLOCK

Cutting the block has always been, for me, the part of block printing that is the most fun. The basic thing to remember in cutting is this: Cut away whatever part of the surface you do not want to be printed. When you have done this, whatever is left in relief will be printed. Practice safety when you are cutting. Grasp the deepest, sharpest gouge firmly and push it away from you through the surface of the linoleum. The hand that is steadying the block on the table must be kept *behind* the cutting point of the gouge to avoid slicing a finger when the tool slips. It invariably does slip until you become accustomed to holding it always at the proper angle. Do not worry if the tool gouges deeply into the linoleum. The deep cut background and canvas backing may even have to be cut away completely before you mount the block.

Practice cutting techniques on linoleum scraps. Wiggle the tool to make jagged lines and fat lines and thin lines. Make stabs at the block, and jabs, to create different textures in the surface. If there

35

are cutting effects that you are not quite sure about, keep scraps of linoleum handy to practice on. Try to feel with the tool the shape that you are outlining, and rout out the background linoleum with lines that will reinforce and strengthen your shapes. Practice making parallel lines as accurately as you can and ending lines with nice square tails, or try to end a line with a smooth, round shape. Circles are difficult to make, as are polka dots, but fun.

If your design is linear or irregularly shaped, you may have a great deal of background that you do not want on the block at all. Outline this area with a deep gouge, then slice it out completely with a knife, razor blade, or scissors. The only exception to this rule is if your design has such fine, delicate lines that they could easily be broken in handling. In this case, cut out only as much of the block as seems reasonable, then wait until the block is mounted before finishing the more intricate cutting.

If you are executing small, delicate patterns or lettering, use a straight knife or a single-edge razor blade for cutting. Cut one side with the blade held at a slight angle, then, reversing the angle, cut out the other side of the channel completely. This technique gives very clean, precise results.

REPAIRING MISTAKES IN CUTTING

It is almost impossible to ruin a block, particularly after you gain control of your tools. But we might as well face it. One sad day the awful thing will happen. Your tool will slip and cut a nick in a vital line. You cannot persuade yourself that the line is not necessary? In that case, you must repair it. This requires rather neat craftsmanship, but it can be done, *after* you finish cutting and mounting the block.

After the block has been mounted, take the deepest, widest V-gouge you have. Make a clean deep cut completely through the line you want to fix at the spot where you made the nick. Now, take a piece of scrap linoleum and, using the same tool, make a similar cut in it. Try to hold the tool at the same angle when making both cuts,

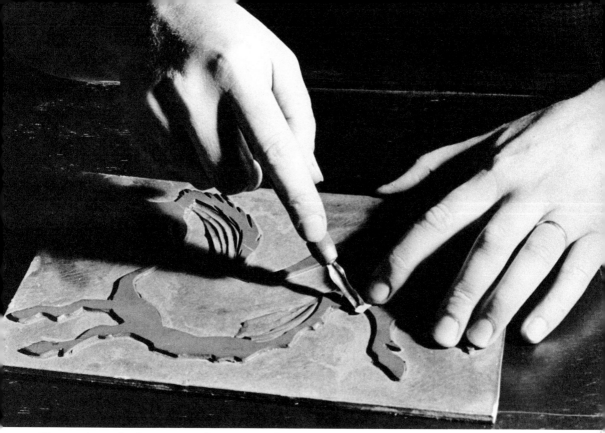

*To repair a mistake, cut out the unwanted area
and match with a small piece of scrap linoleum*

Glue the repair piece in place, and trim it to conform with the original line

and keep the depth of the cuts the same. Set this piece you have just gouged out into the broken line. With luck it will be a perfect fit. It can be glued into place and trimmed to conform to the original line.

To repair larger areas in a block it is usually best, and easiest, to cut out the whole section around the part you want to repair. When mounting the block on the backing you can replace this section with a new, uncut piece of linoleum. Use the cut-out piece as a pattern to arrive at the proper shape for this new section. The design can now be re-cut to match the rest of the block.

After you have cut your design almost completely out, you may have some doubts as to what it will look like when it is finally printed. To test your design, hold your block to a mirror. If the mirror image looks balanced, then you are probably ready to print.

CUTTING THE BACKING

Gouging out the design will make the linoleum quite floppy. It should now be mounted upon a piece of backing so that you will be able to handle it easily when printing.

Measure and mark off the section of backing that you will need. It should be big enough to support all the parts of your design. Check the size by laying the cut linoleum on the area you have marked off. Then, using the steel-edge ruler as a guide, score the lines with a knife or single-edge razor blade. Do not try to cut completely through on the first try. Keep the steel edge in the same position and pull the blade along the scored line several times, until you have cut completely and cleanly through.

GLUEING THE BACKING

Trace the outline of the cut design onto the backing so you will know where to apply the glue. Using a small scrap of cardboard, fill in the outline with a thin coat of glue. Now, put some glue on the back of the design. The backing and the reverse side of the linoleum are absorbent surfaces, so both must be coated with glue to assure a good bond.

38

If you are using water-soluble liquid glue, coat both surfaces as described and let them dry for fifteen minutes or until tacky. This seals the surfaces. Then apply another coat of glue to the back of the linoleum and press it onto the backing board. Wrap the mounted block in a fold of newspaper and place it between flat boards under pressure to set. A three gallon pail of water makes a good weight, or you could use a pair of heavy book ends. If the block is not under pressure as it sets, the moisture in the glue will warp the backing board out of shape, and the bond of the linoleum to the backing will be weak. After the block has been set, usually in four to six hours, excess glue that has been squeezed from the block under pressure can be scrubbed from the face of the mounted block with warm water and a bristle brush. Apply horsehide, fish, and rabbitskin glue in the same way, but allow these twelve hours to set.

SHELLACKING THE BLOCK

Any exposed paper board area on the face of the block should be shellacked. Then, if any ink is accidentally rolled, dropped, or spattered onto this background, it can easily be wiped off the non-absorbent shellac. The back of the block should also be protected in this way to keep the cardboard from absorbing water from the damp fabric. Blocks that are not protected with shellac will warp and shred from exposure to this wetness.

It is a good idea to mark the top and bottom of the design on the back of the block. This is easiest to do before the backing has been shellacked. Marking the back of the block eliminates the possibility of placing a block upside down on the fabric.

PRINTING BY FOOT

Printing is not only simple in theory, it is easy to do. The idea is to coat the block with ink, place it face down on the surface to be printed, and apply pressure. The ink is transferred under pressure from the block to the blank surface, which is "imprinted" with an exact, although reversed, reproduction of the image on the block.

The simplest and most direct way to apply pressure in block printing

The simplest and most direct way of applying pressure to anything is to step on it. This is the method I use in my studio, and one which I teach to my students. Not only does it give even, uniform prints, but it is the most practical way to print large bedspreads, tablecloths, drapery panels, and wall hangings.

Dancers' light-soled practice slippers make fine block printing shoes, and so do sneakers. You can feel the edges of the block through the sole. However, I usually work barefoot.

MAKING A PRINTING BED

To make a temporary printing bed, select a wide, flat section of floor. Any place providing sufficient floor space will do. It is best if this place is well lighted. It should also be free of lumps and hollows and large enough to allow you to stretch your textile out to its full length. If it is carpeted, so much the better, as long as the carpet has no seams. Or you can lay the bed directly on the bare floor, sweeping it first to make sure there are no bits of dirt or grit to make lumps under the padding.

Building a printing bed by laying out separate sheets of newspaper

You will need a collection of newspapers to build up a thick blanket of padding. To pad a bed four by eight feet you should start with a pile about six inches high. Each piece of paper should be laid out separately. Do not attempt to lay the papers out in bunches because this will make a bed with distressing humps and hollows. Instead, separate each sheet and lay it flat, slightly overlapping the others already spread. Build up quite a thick pad in this way, smoothing it as you build by stepping on it gently. The purpose of the newspapers is to provide a soft pad on which to print. Printing on something soft gives you a more solid print, since any slight irregularities on the surface of your block do not show up. The pad also acts as a blotter, absorbing excess water and holding it so that the fabric has the right degree of dampness as you print.

If you are printing more than one piece, lay some clean sheets of newspaper on top of the bed after you have taken up each completed length. Otherwise you may stain your new fabric with inks that have leaked through from a previous printing. Do not try to save the newspapers to print upon again, since newspaper, once wet, gets crumpled and wrinkled. If you should use a rug as a base, make sure you lay enough newspapers so that the inks will not penetrate. If you do make spots on your rug or floor, wipe them up instantly with kerosene or turpentine.

A permanent printing surface is a great convenience because you do not need to spend a lot of time laying down a thick padding of newspapers each time you want to print. Also, it holds firmly the T-pins with which you stretch your fabric. It can easily be raised from the floor to table height on chairs or saw horses, eliminating the need for a lot of bending while stretching, measuring, and pinning the wet fabric.

Homasote, a cheap wallboard that comes in four by eight and four by ten foot sheets, is a very good printing surface. It is light and can be easily handled by one person and stored upright against a wall when not in use. The soft surface takes T-pins easily and holds them firmly. It is rigid enough to equalize any uneven spots that might exist in the floor. A four by eight foot panel costs three and a half dollars.

You can also make a permanent bed from a four by eight foot panel of one-quarter or one-half inch plywood. It can be permanently padded with cotton felting or an old blanket, protected by a covering of oilcloth or plastic. Both padding and covering should be stretched tight and smooth and fastened firmly to the underside of the bed with staples or tacks. Such a bed can be made for about seven dollars. You can buy cotton felting in a tailor's supply store.

A Homasote panel or a plywood bed padded with blanketing and oilcloth will need several layers of paper laid down before you spread the wet fabric, to make a blotting layer between the fabric and the non-absorbent covering.

The four by eight foot bed will be large enough for most projects that you will be undertaking. Occasionally, however, you may want to print a wide tablecloth, or a bedspread, or even an unusually long drapery panel. If feasible and convenient, you could build a wider and longer bed. Plywood is available in larger panels than four by eight feet, but it is considerably more expensive than in the standard size sheet.

If you plan only one or two extra large projects, it is best to improvise. You could stretch out as much of your length as will fit onto the bed, print that section, and then move the fabric and re-stretch it to print the rest. Or you could clear a large section of flat floor and lay a big newspaper bed. I sometimes print in a large garage with a concrete floor. This creates some difficulties because I cannot pin into the floor, but it is possible to make colossal size block prints, if you can adapt yourself gracefully to such limitations.

Newsprint is a convenience when printing. Whether you are working with a temporary or permanent bed, it is an advantage if you can cover the newspapers with some clean, *blank* newsprint. This can be bought in pads from an art supply store or in a roll from a wholesale paper company. A single sheet of clean top padding makes it much easier to mark off measurements and seam points and easier, too, to see them. A roll about twelve inches in diameter should cost about ten dollars and should last for a long time.

Let me repeat, newsprint is a convenience but not a necessity. It is possible to print directly on the newspapers, without any clean top layer, and I have worked this way many times, as have many of my students. Newsprint will be necessary *only* when you are printing on light color silk. This is discussed more fully in the section on Special Projects, under *Scarves*.

PRINTING BY HAND AND BY MECHANICAL PRESS

There is an alternative to the foot pressure method of block printing that has been used successfully by many craftsmen. Instead of stepping on the block to make an impression, they pound the back of it with a mallet or hammer. A rubber automobile repairman's mallet is recommended because it makes less noise than a wood or metal-headed hammer. The size of the length you can conveniently print this way is rather limited, but it is a good way to print smaller things.

For printing by hand, a newspaper bed is laid on a table top at convenient working height, and the wet fabric is spread out in the way already described. The blocks also are prepared and inked in the same way and laid face down on the fabric. Then the back of the block is struck with the mallet, all sections being covered just as they would be if you were stepping on the block. It helps when printing a large block to lay a piece of wood slightly larger than the block over it before you start pounding. The wood, being more rigid than the cardboard backing of the block, will equalize the force from the blows of the mallet, thus helping to make more even prints.

Some craftsmen prefer to use hand presses. There are several types suitable for block printing on fabric. Because of the limited printing area, they are best adapted for printing small projects.

45

PART

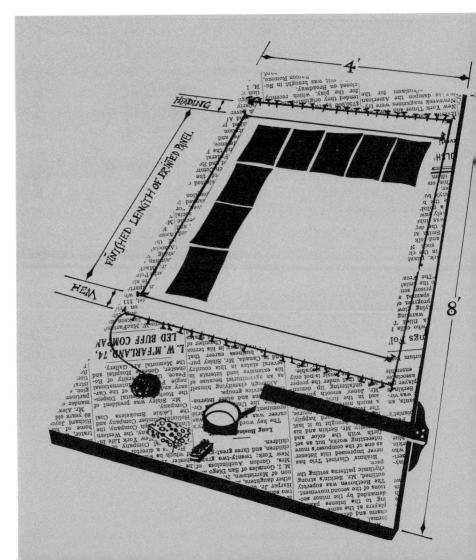

3 *Printing the Block*

CHOOSING A FABRIC

FABRIC IS A WONDROUSLY VARIED INVENTION OF MAN. It is fine, soft, and silken or so rough and prickly that it repels your hand. It can be tightly impenetrable or a gossamer web stirred by a breath. It is animal, vegetable, and now mineral. It is usually made by interlacing threads in a simple pattern, but it can be pounded from fluffy balls of unspun fiber.

Because you will be spending time and energy making and printing your design, you will want to choose the kind of fabric that will be most appropriate for your project, and one that has beauty in itself. To guide you in selecting the types of fabric you want to use, a list of the common fibers and some of the characteristics of the cloths into which they are made is included in the back of the book.

When buying fabric to block print always get enough extra to allow for the shrinkage that may take place when it is washed before printing. Some inexpensive cottons may shrink as much as four inches in a yard. You will also need a small extra piece to make a test print on. The test prints will show you how your color scheme will

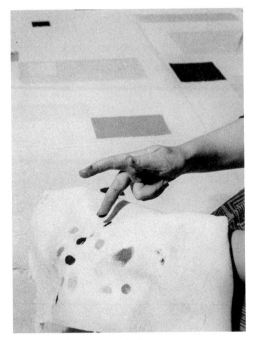

The texture of the fabric combined with the design of your block can create greater pattern interest

A test print on a fabric scrap will give you an idea of the ultimate effect

look. Also you can see if your ink is the right consistency for the kind of fabric you have.

Never try to *think* out a color scheme. Always try it first on a scrap of the color fabric it is to be printed upon. Mix up a small amount of ink in approximately the same color, or colors, that you are thinking of using. Take a bit of this ink on the tip of the finger and rub it into the scrap piece. Be sure to rub the ink well into the cloth. Dropping a heavy glob of ink onto the surface of the fabric and letting it dry there will not tell you what the ink color will be when printed onto the fabric and absorbed into the fibers. Ink printed on fabric is affected not only by the color of the fabric but by its texture as well. So rub it in well, and give it a chance to dry. A minute should be enough. Then look at your scrap in daylight so that you can see its true color. Most artificial light is quite yellowish and will change the ink color effects considerably, particularly in the blue and green range.

Keep in mind that very fine lines hold up best on smooth silky fabrics, while large solid areas of printed color are most successful on heavy fabrics. The thick layer of ink needed for a solid print does not as completely fill and stiffen a heavily textured fabric as it does a lighter one.

MEASURING AND CUTTING FABRIC

Having chosen a length of fabric suitable for your project in a color that is pleasing to you and in a texture that complements your design, you must now cut it to the proper size and shape for printing. First, it must be squared up. Squaring a length makes certain that there are exactly as many weft, or crosswise, threads along one selvage as along the other and, of course, in the center of the piece. When the length is spread on the bed you will be able to draw straight lines and make accurate measurements, knowing that as you stretch the fabric to conform to these lines, you are not forcing it to an unnatural shape that it will refuse to keep when dry.

Each raw edge must be straightened by cutting it along a thread. The selvage, which is the woven edge at either side of the piece, is, of course, a straight edge. If your piece has been torn, not cut, from selvage to selvage, it will be square because fabric almost invariably tears along a thread. If the fabric does not tear easily, do not force it. With a pair of scissors nip into the selvage near the raw edge you want to square up. Use a common pin to separate one thread out from the others. Pull on this one thread and slide it out of the cloth. Depending on the weave of the fabric it will come readily

Pull threads to show cutting line

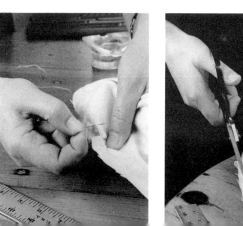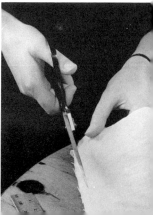

or with difficulty. Threads can be pulled easily from loosely woven goods. Fine linen threads can scarcely be pulled at all. As the thread slides from the cloth it will leave a line for you to follow in cutting.

If the fabric is a very finely woven one, pulling the threads may prove to be an impossibly time-consuming job. In this case, you could make your measurements along one selvage and along one end, putting in a small safety pin at each point instead of nipping the fabric. When the length is spread on the bed, you can stretch strings from these pins across the piece to indicate the size of each piece. Of course the ends must be squared as usual.

When measuring cloth, do not put tension on it. Hold it flat and evenly spread out, *but under no strain*.

When you cut your fabric, always remember to add a generous allowance for shrinkage. Some inexpensive cottons and linens that have not been treated for "crush resistance" generally shrink quite a lot. Those that have been so treated do not. Silk shrinks somewhat and rayons usually quite a lot. When in doubt about a particular fabric, make a test.

Cut your fabric into lengths convenient to handle. You can waste a lot of time laying out, measuring, and pinning down individual small pieces of fabric. If you are printing cocktail napkins, placemats, or even drapery lengths it is easier to leave several short pieces in one length, pulling a thread to indicate the division lines. Fabric for draperies should be cut into lengths that are convenient sizes to work on but not so long as to be too heavy to handle when wet.

DE-SIZING THE FABRIC

All fabrics while being woven are more or less heavily sized. This starch sizing is added to the individual thread as it is fed onto the loom. Sized threads do not break so readily on the loom as unsized, and cloth woven with sized threads has a stiff feel, a "good hand." This sizing is soluble in water and rinses from the fabric the first time the length is washed.

If your block print has been made on heavily sized cloth, it will fade noticeably in the first washing. To avoid this, the fabric must be de-sized by soaking it for a few minutes in a pail of lukewarm water. As the fabric is always block printed wet, this de-sizing process can sometimes be combined with the preliminary soaking.

Some fabrics are loaded with sizing. Examples are such fabrics as muslin and other inexpensive cotton cloths like bagging (sometimes called osnaberg), the pebble weaves, and some bark cloths. A fabric of this type must be thoroughly washed before printing. Put each length through your washing machine, or soak it overnight in a tub with a strong detergent powder to loosen the sizing, and rinse it thoroughly.

LAYING OUT THE FABRIC

First draw a line across the bed near one end. A string stretched from one side of the bed to the other makes a straight line that is easy to see. Push a T-pin firmly into the bed, wind the string around it and pull tightly across to another T-pin to get a straight line.

Then, lift your fabric dripping from the water in which it has been soaking. Squeeze it gently to expel some of the water, but do not wring it. You want it quite wet when it goes onto the bed. The layers of absorbent newspapers will drink up the excess water and hold it, keeping the fabric damp as you work on it.

Laying out the fabric

51

*Smoothing the fabric out on the bed, easing the top end
out to its natural width before pinning it*

Smooth the damp fabric out on the bed, easing the top end out
to what seems to be its natural width. Do not stretch it; as it is damp,
it can easily be pulled out of shape. Pin the top edge to your straight
line, using a pin every inch or so.

Smooth the fabric out to its full length and pin the bottom edge
to another line. Make careful measurements and try to keep your
fabric square on the bed. Pull the selvages out toward the sides of
the bed, and smooth them down with a wet sponge. Do not pin
these edges.

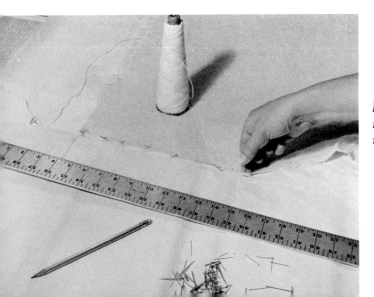

*Pinning the top edge to the line
indicated by the string,
using a T-pin every inch or so*

Placing dummy blocks on the fabric as guides
for the design and printing

Stretch another string across the fabric to show where you want to place the edges of your blocks in printing. Or cut out of scrap paper half a dozen shapes exactly the same size as your block. Place a row of these dummies across the fabric where your first prints will be made. Adjust the placement until it is just as you want it. Remember to plan not only how the blocks will fit into the width of the fabric, but how they will fit into the length. The dummies can be left in place and removed as you make your prints. If laid out accurately they will help keep your prints properly lined up.

You can also use a string to indicate where hems turn up on draperies and skirts or to mark the division lines between individual mats or napkins when working with fabrics in which it is difficult to pull out a thread.

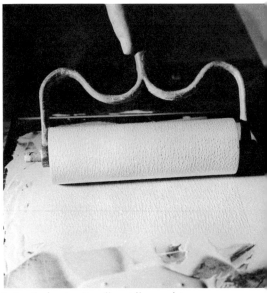

Loosening stiff ink with a drop of linseed oil

Ink of the proper "snap" consistency rolled out thoroughly on the palette

LAYING OUT THE INK

If the ink seems stiff when it comes from the tube or can, loosen it with a drop of boiled linseed oil. Too much ink will make the oil spread or "bleed" along the fibers of the cloth. When you think the ink has a proper consistency, gather it into a compact pile in one corner of your palette and clean up the rest of the palette surface. Dip your brayer into this pile and transfer a small amount of ink to the center of the palette. Roll this ink out thoroughly. The ink should "snap" and look as if it were full of tiny air bubbles. If it is still too stiff, add more linseed oil, carefully, one drop at a time.

Sometimes when you lay out ink that has been used before, you will find lumps of dried ink or "skin" mixed with it. Lift out the larger of these lumps and discard them. Watch your brayer carefully to see that no lumps get on it to be transferred to the block. If you have a batch of very lumpy, dirty ink, you can strain it.

Always keep your ink separated on the palette into two distinct sections, the flattened brayed-out part that you are using and the pile of extra ink. Keeping the extra ink in a compact pile helps to prevent it from drying out before you are ready to use it and also makes it easier to control the amount of ink you get on the brayer each time you roll it through the ink.

Always prepare more ink than you think you will need. It is better to have some left over than to have to try to match a color in order to finish out one or two prints. Ink can always be saved and used again.

INKING THE BLOCK

When you ink the block, the area of the table around it may get messy with ink and some of this ink may be transferred onto the back of the block. To prevent this, lay a section of folded newspapers next to the palette and place the block face up on them. When the top sheet becomes sticky with ink, rip it off and work on a clean surface.

Roll the brayer back and forth through the ink so that the roller is evenly covered; then roll it gently over the surface of the block. Do not put any pressure on it or you will force the ink into lowered background areas which you do not wish to print. You may have to ink the brayer and roll it over the block several times to cover it completely. When you have finished, hold the block up sideways to the light to see if you have left any sections un-inked.

If you have a little too much ink on your brayer, some of the excess may have run over the sides of the block. Run your forefinger along the sides to wipe it off. If there is ink on any of the background that you do not want to print, wipe it off with a dry rag.

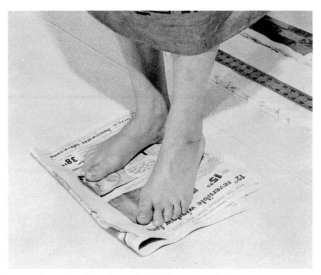

Covering the block and fabric around it
with newspaper keeps the fabric clean

PRINTING THE BLOCK

Holding the block carefully by the edges, place it face down on the fabric. To keep the fabric clean, cover the block and the fabric around it with a sheet of clean newspaper. Now, with your toes, tramp gently all over the back of the block. As your instep is higher than your toe or heel, it will not transfer any pressure to the block.

When printing a large block, begin at one side, pressing on one section at a time, then move across to the other side. Do not go back over the section just printed, as the block may have shifted slightly. You would blur the image if you put pressure on that section again. Keep one foot solidly on the block to prevent it from sliding on the fabric while you move the other foot.

Never shift the block after placing it on the fabric. Once it has touched the fabric you must go ahead and print it. It will often turn out that it is not so far off as you imagined. And even if it is definitely out of line, do not despair. Fabrics are usually draped, and mistakes tend to disappear in the folds.

56

Now, step carefully off the block. Remove the newspaper and lift the block straight up. Standing it on one edge as you lift it will blur that edge. Your print should have clear, distinct edges and well-covered solid areas. Remember that the fabric is wet and will be slightly lighter in color when it dries.

If there are some blank spots in your print, it may be that your ink is too stiff, or your brayer might not be rotating properly in its handle. Perhaps your fabric is too damp or too dry. Look at the block to see if extra ink is left on the part of the design that is not clear in the impression. You may not have stood on that spot care-

Lift the block straight up to avoid blurring the ink

fully enough. A little experience will teach you to make a quick diagnosis and correct any difficulties.

REPAIRING MISTAKES IN PRINTING

If your block makes a very light, indistinct impression, you may need to print it over again. This is possible but it must be done carefully. It can only be done when the edge of the design coincides with the edge of the block in at least two places. Ink the block, and replace it over the first print as accurately as you can, matching up all the points that you can see. An assistant can help by watching one side of the block while you concentrate on the other side.

You can easily repair small empty spots in the print. You will need a toothpick or the sharpened wooden end of a paintbrush. Dip the point of your stick into the ink and tamp the point onto the spot you want to fill in. Tamp straight down. Do not try to brush the ink onto the spot. This would only ruffle the surface fibers of the cloth. Fill in the hole a bit at a time, always using an up and down motion.

Small, unprinted areas are easily repaired

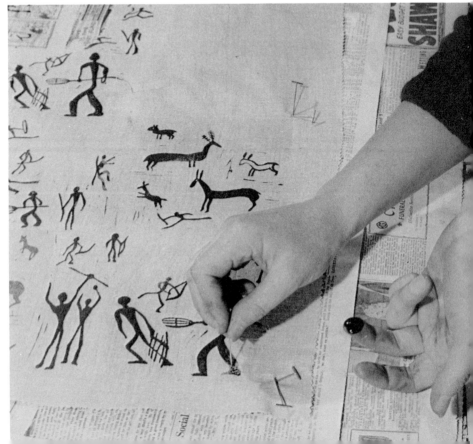

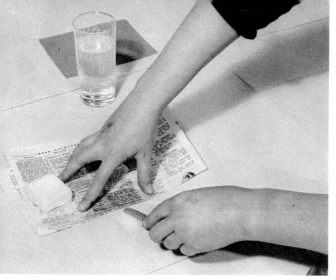

Careful scrubbing removes fingerprints and spots

Inky finger prints and other small accidental spots should be removed from the fabric as soon as possible. To wash them out you will need a stiff bristle brush, a bar of strong soap, a piece of celluloid or thin cardboard, and a pan of water. An old tooth brush is a good scrub brush, as it is small enough to get at the tiniest spots. Lay the cardboard so that it completely covers and protects any print that is close to the spot. Then, wet the brush and rub it over the bar of soap until it lathers. Now scrub away at the spot, using a rotary motion. You will need to scrub quite hard so that you raise a lather. When the spot seems to be gone, rinse the brush in clean water and flush the soapy lather from the fabric with more clean water. This treatment should work with all but the heaviest spots. If you are not satisfied with the results of the first scrubbing, repeat the process.

The scrubbing technique is a bit rough on the fabric and should be used very carefully on fine, light textures. On silks, organdies, and similar delicate weaves it is better to correct mistakes and spots by inventing an addition to the design that can be printed over the unwanted spot. Often a simple square or triangle that you can cut out of a scrap of linoleum with scissors will be most effective.

Corrections should be made as soon as possible. Try to remove spots and make any repairs that are needed while the piece is still spread out on the bed. It is easy to do the job effectively then, and it usually takes only a few additional minutes. For a misprint that can be fixed in no other way, you might consider a spot of decorative embroidery or appliqué that will complement your design.

Reprinting the block makes the textile design

FROM BLOCK PRINT INTO TEXTILE DESIGN

Your first single print shows you your single design by itself. Ink it up again and print it once more right beside the first impression. Now print it again and again. The block must be inked each time that it is printed. These repeating prints will bring out elements in the design that could not be seen in it as a single unit. Rhythmic lines will develop, and unsuspected areas will emerge as you build up an area of prints. Your print is becoming a TEXTILE DESIGN.

Now that you know what your design looks like printed in a straightforward way, you can experiment by printing your block in various combinations to produce a checkerboard repeat, a half-drop, or overprints. Print the block without inking it once or twice to see

The first single print shows your design

what the lighter image looks like juxtaposed to the solid print. You can have no idea of the possibilities inherent in your design until you have reprinted it many times in many different arrangements and in many different color combinations.

You can use one color by itself or combine a rainbow in a single block. Start out boldly planning the colors for your block print. Before deciding on a combination, experiment with improbable hues to develop your awareness of what unusual colors can do for your design. Observe the daring and wonderful color schemes of nature and learn to rely on your own judgment.

Ink it and print it

62

Print the block without inking it
to see what the lighter image looks like
juxtaposed to the solid print

Checkerboard repeat

64

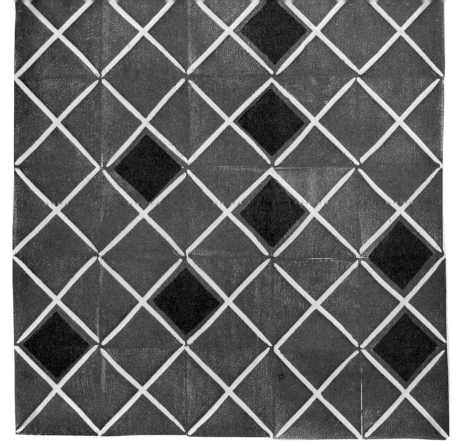

Overprints

Half-drop

You can add richness to a simple one-block design by printing it in two colors. Make the first print in one color, the second in another. Or you might use a light and a dark value of the same color. Use a separate brayer for each color. It is not necessary to clean your block as you change back and forth from color to color.

A ONE-BLOCK DESIGN INKED AND PRINTED CONSECUTIVELY IN THREE HARMONIZING COLORS CREATES A RICH, OFF-REGISTER PATTE

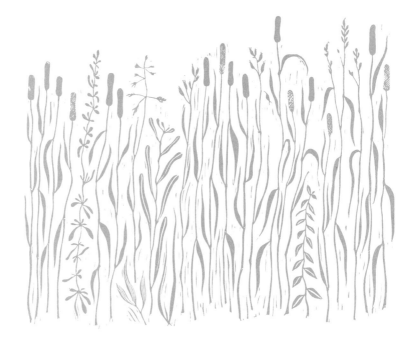

first color

second color

third color

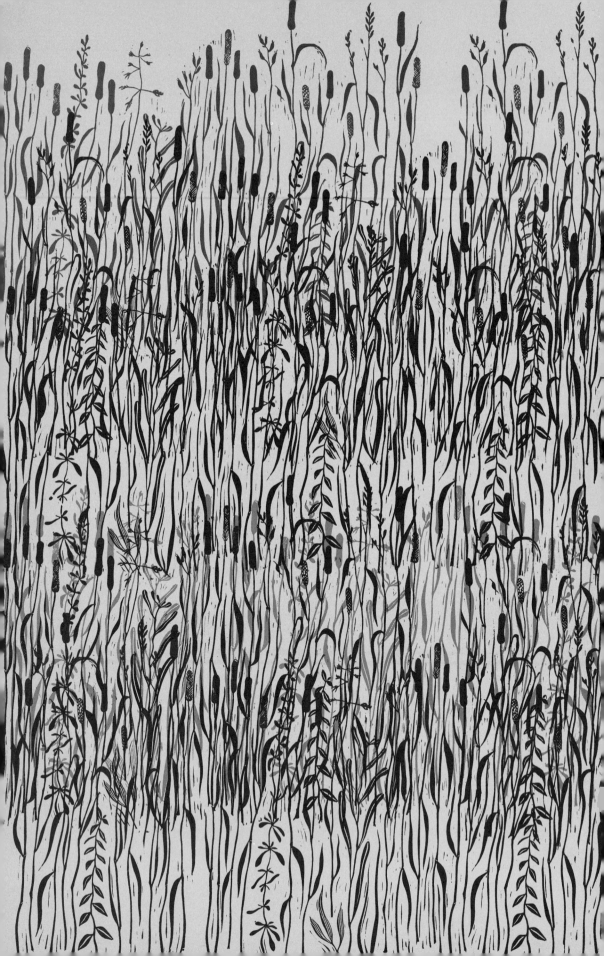

final print

Blending two colors on the block is another way to get a multi-color effect with a single block. Use three brayers, one for each color and a narrow one to blend the area where the colors meet. Make a few practice prints to learn how much ink to use. The blending brayer must be used with a light hand.

Color elements can sometimes be combined in a single printing. For example, if you have a block with several areas on it that are separated from each other by two or three inches, you can ink one area in one color and one in a second color to get a variety of color elements with a single printing. Use a pounce to ink small spots of color inside solid areas of another color.

*Inking two colors on a single block
can produce interesting harmonies — Stell and Shevis*

Interesting value contrasts can be achieved by printing a design
in alternating negative and positive blocks

Contrasts in value and intensity also create pleasing combinations. The *value* of a color, its lightness or darkness, depends on how much white or black it contains. *Intensity* is the brightness or grayness of a color and varies according to how much pure pigment a color contains. Contrasts in the value and intensity of a color are more important in creating pleasing combinations that contrasts from one color to another. For instance, hunter's green and royal blue are

70

Sensitive combinations of high and low contrast require car
planning — Freda Hall Lipmann

similar, quite intense colors of about the same value. Together they produce a dull effect. Lighten the value of the green to a pale pastel shade and the result is a lively combination of contrasting values. Take the same green and the same blue, but this time reduce the intensity of the blue, making it almost a gray. Keep it the same value. The contrast in intensity will create a rich, subdued effect.

Consider also the proportions of color areas in planning combinations. A very bright color that would be garish and tasteless printed all over a fabric can often be used with striking effect as an accent spot. And, a color that seems dull in a test square is sometimes handsome when printed over a larger area.

Colors can brighten or neutralize each other. As you gain experience you will learn that you can add to the brilliance of a bright color by surrounding it with gray tones. Also, when you use bright colors side by side they will tend to neutralize each other. Each will seem duller than when used alone.

High intensity colors should be used carefully. When complementary colors of high intensity and similar value are placed side by side, they vibrate. The edges of the color spots become blurred and dance around. A fabric printed in these colors would be striking, but not very soothing to live with.

Contrasting a print color with the fabric color creates a strong effect. To state a very general rule: you can create strongly contrasting color combinations by printing intense, dark colors (e.g., maroon, chocolate brown, navy blue, deep green) on very light or white fabrics. And very light, bright colors (white, lemon yellow, vermilion, turquoise) will contrast effectively with dark backgrounds. Printing with color that is only slightly lighter or darker than the fabric, however, can create a very subtle effect.

No ink is completely opaque. Even with cover white you can never print a true white on a dark background. The printed white will always take on somewhat the color of the background. If you want to print your design in strong, true, brilliant colors, start with a white background fabric.

A single block can achieve quite varied effects when printed in contrasting inks on different surfaces (in this case paper and silk) — Freda Hall Lipmann

In planning your color, consider the *texture* as well as the *color* of the fabric you are printing on. White will seem whiter printed on a stiff, shiny dark green taffeta which does not absorb much ink than it will on the same shade of dark green felt with a very absorbent surface.

You can completely change the effect of a design by changing colors and fabric. A design printed in soft gray-green ink on chartreuse silk would look very different if printed upon heavy white linen in magenta ink.

A linear design can be made more dramatic by printing it first in one color then printing it over again in a strongly contrasting color. This creates a shadowed, slightly off-register look.

You can also print in broad strips or blocks of alternating colors. Some designs are handsome with the strips kept clean and separate; others are most effective with areas of colors overlapping.

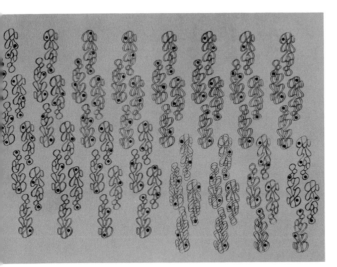

A shadow effect produced by printing the block a second time slightly off register. A pencil eraser made the dotted accents
— *Barbara Hunt*

Imaginative changes in the position, value, and sequence of individual blocks create an interesting design

74

*Overlapping blocks of varied values
and colors create an effective design*

INTRODUCING FREE ELEMENTS
INTO YOUR DESIGN

The regular repetition of design elements makes a traditional textile pattern. But it is also possible to repeat elements while varying their arrangement. Try printing some of your blocks to make a non-repeating pattern. A non-repeat design is simply one in which elements are used in a continuously varied arrangement of shapes or colors, without losing a sense of unified design.

To give depth of color to a simple all over pattern, you can add printed areas of solid color to the background. Cut geometrical or free-form shapes from linoleum, scraps of tile, wood, or cardboard. These shapes can be printed first or added after the over-all design is complete. Areas of color used freely can also help to tie unrelated design elements together.

EXAMPLES OF FOUND TEXTURES

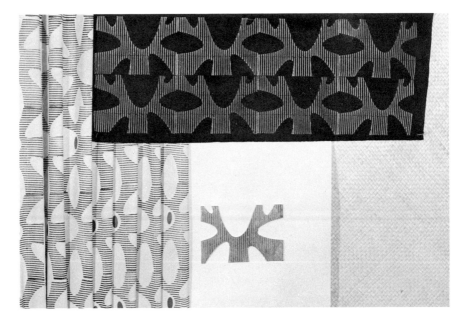

A block cut from corrugated cardboard can be printed in effective combinations of pattern and value

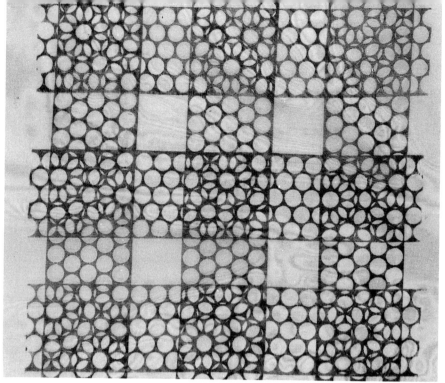

*An ordinary gasket mounted on cardboard
prints like a linoleum block — Hazen Wolfe*

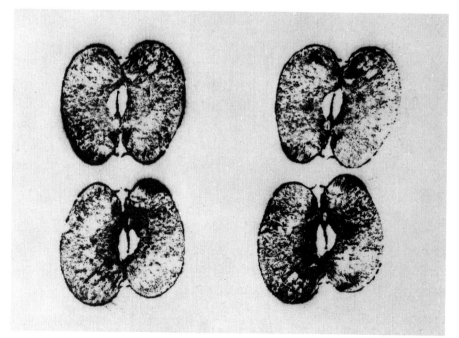

Placemat printed directly with apple halves

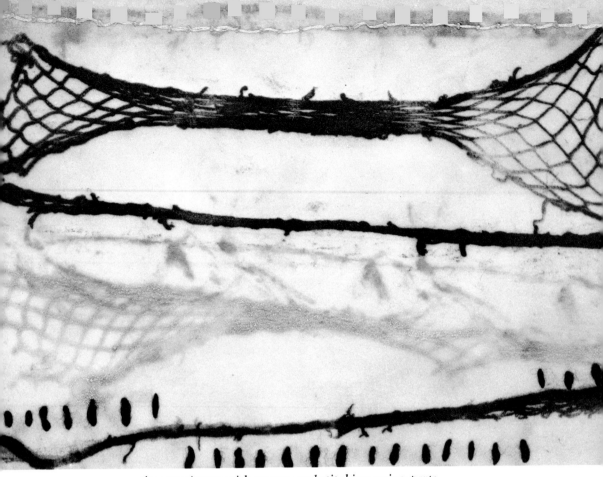

An experiment with texture and stitching, using parts of a hair net on sponge rubber — Caroline Hoskyns

You might also try printing from "found textures" to build up the effect you want. You can "find" textures anywhere. Look for an object that has enough surface irregularity to take ink in a printable pattern. A section of cardboard with exposed corrugations can be inked just as you would ink a block. A coat of shellac makes it last longer. A sponge always gives a delightful texture. It should be used damp. Lay the sponge on the flat ink section of your palette and press down gently. Then lay it on the fabric and again press down with your hand. Experiment to see exactly how hard to press. Laces and meshes of all kinds can be used, as can bricks, bones, buttons, and bare feet. Your kitchen is full of objects waiting to be "found." In fact, you can print with practically everything but the kitchen sink.

78

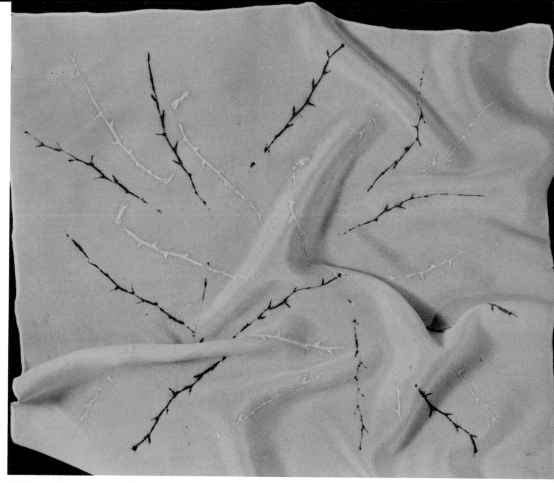

Silk scarf printed with inked twigs — Joan Bird

*Printing directly with grass
and twigs — Sterling McIlhany*

79

An airy effect is easy to achieve with a stencil and a sprayer

A "found texture" cannot be controlled too precisely. This is part of its charm. You must decide how much texture is effective and where it can be used best. Often a found texture can be used to best effect as a more or less random background contrasting with a more precisely realized design printed over it.

For a loose textural color effect, roll the ink directly onto the fabric with your brayer. Be careful not to get so much ink on the fabric that it becomes stiff. You can get a quite different effect by placing an object with a definite, strong texture under the fabric before rolling the brayer over it.

Varied decorative effects can be achieved also by using a stencil with a brayer. Cut an interestingly shaped hole in a large sheet of heavy, stiff paper. Place it on the fabric and run your ink-covered brayer over the hole. The ink will print through the hole. Or you could make solid shapes, pin them to the fabric, and run your brayer around the outside of these. For an airy effect, spray thin ink through a stencil or spatter ink from a stiff brush.

80

A set of separate, registered blocks is required
to print this lively, multicolored drapery design

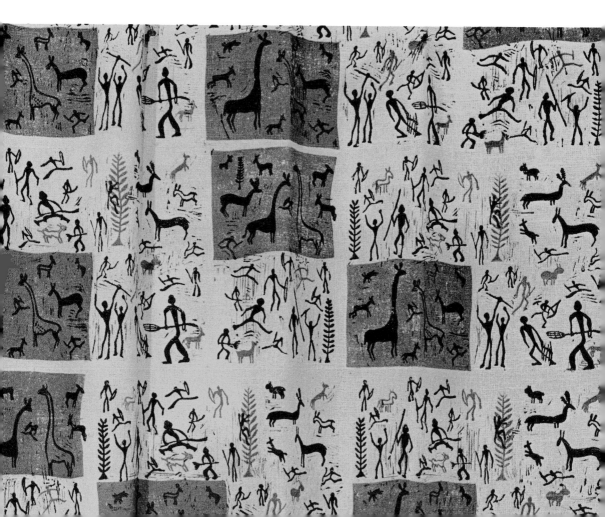

MAKING A REGISTERED BLOCK

To print multi-colored designs with definite areas of color one over the other, you need a set of separate, registered blocks. A different block is usually required for each large area of color. Small color accents can sometimes be mounted on a single block and printed all at once.

First, make a sketch of approximately what you want your final design to look like. Work out the placing of color areas quite carefully. A set of pastels is useful in making this kind of color sketch, or shapes cut out of colored cellophane can help you to visualize the way one area will look when printed over another.

Now, decide which block will have the most detail on it. It will be your key block. Plan how many other blocks you will need for the color effects you want. You can make as many blocks as you think you will need, but remember that each additional block means another printing. Next, outline a rectangle, square, or triangle that will contain all the parts of your design. Cut a sheet of backing exactly this shape and size for each block you will need. The corners must be very accurately cut because you will use them as guides in printing.

Then, cut the design of your key block and mount it on a piece of backing, and glue a second piece of linoleum to another backing. Make a very wet print of the key block on a sheet of paper (plain newsprint is best). Carefully mark around the corners of the block before picking it up.

Now, place the second block face down on this wet print, using the corner marks as guides to place it exactly where the other block was. Tramp on it so that the wet print will off-set onto it. You can now cut the parts of the design on this second block to match those on the key block.

Sometimes you can save linoleum by making an offset print on the backing sheet and mounting pieces of linoleum on the backing only at those places where the design appears on this block.

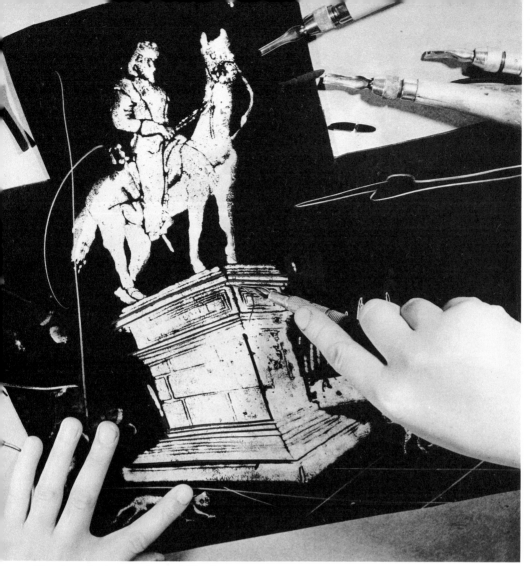

Carving the last registered block

The final effect

Top: *The largest color area used in the design serves as a basis for the key block, which is printed in yellow. The orange accents are simply rolled onto the key block with a separate brayer*

REGISTERED BLOCKS ARE USED TO CREATE A PLACEMAT

Bottom: *For final detail and added emphasis the second registered block is printed in black over the key block*

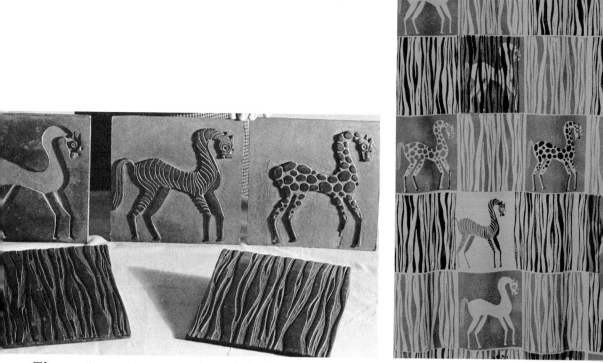

*The use of more than two registered blocks of contrasting values
produces a rich, almost three-dimensional surface.
Varied combinations of the registered blocks
lend liveliness to this drapery*

WORKING TECHNIQUES FOR CRAFTSMEN

The first print on a length is always the most exciting, but the last one is the most satisfying. If possible, try to finish a length in one printing session. If you do have to stop for a few minutes, clean the extra ink from your block, scrape the ink on your palette into a small pile, and clean your brayer. As short a time as half an hour can make your ink dry and gummy and leave your brayer tacky.

When you are cleaning a block in order to re-ink it with another color right away, do not clean the block with kerosene or turpentine. These solvents get into the lines of the block, and, as they do not dry out quickly, often leave the lines moist for several hours afterward. When you roll ink over the block, the solvent will attack it near the moist lines and make a very messy print. Wipe the block thoroughly with a clean, dry rag and brush the lines carefully with a clean, dry scrub brush.

If necessary, you can leave an unfinished length on the bed overnight or even longer. It is not a good idea to take an unfinished piece up from the bed. No matter how careful you may be, it is almost impossible to stretch fabric exactly the same way twice. Your measurements and plans for registering will have to be done over.

If you are planning to print several similar lengths and want to finish them to a uniform size, as with a series of drapery panels, you should make a quick diagram, noting the exact measurements that you have used on the first panel. Measurements are easily forgotten, and wet fabric can stretch to a confusing number of lengths.

THE FABRIC AFTER PRINTING

When completed, the length should be unpinned and hung as soon as possible. Bits of newspaper may cling to the back of heavily printed areas when a piece has been allowed to dry on the bed. They are difficult to soak off after the print has set.

The wet length should be hung over a clothesline strung overhead in an out of the way corner of your work space. Prints made with oil base block printing inks should dry in the air for five days. The ink will be surface dry after two or three days, depending on atmospheric conditions, and if necessary the piece can be gently folded flat and allowed to finish drying on a shelf.

After the printed length has dried on the line or on the shelf for five days, it must be color set. If the length is a short one, or if you have printed on a thin, fast drying fabric, it can be completely dipped in a mixture of vinegar and water, in proportion about one teaspoonful of vinegar to a quart of water. A momentary but thorough immersion is enough. It can then drip dry until it reaches the degree of dryness at which the particular fabric is most efficiently ironed. It should then be pressed on the reverse side of the print with an iron set at the proper heat for the fabric. As you press it you will see the color penetrate more deeply into the fiber.

If your piece is a long one, or if the fabric is a linen or a thick slow-drying texture, it is easiest to sponge it with the vinegar mixture as you press it. This will save a long wait for the fabric to damp dry and an interminable time pressing it to dryness.

THE INKS AFTER PRINTING

Any clean, leftover ink should be scraped up, put in a can, sealed with water or linseed oil, and saved to be used another time. Some fabrics have a great deal of lint which the block will pick up and transfer to the brayer as you roll the block. From the brayer it gets mixed in with the ink on the palette. This linty ink should be discarded. It is not worth saving and will only spoil whatever fresh ink is mixed in with it.

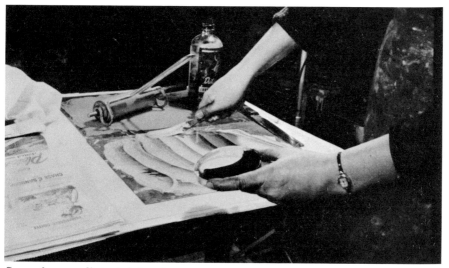

Save clean, unlinty ink for future use

You should start right away to collect old tuna fish or frozen fruit juice cans for "base" cans. By storing left-over ink in these cans, you can always save the excess for another day. Moreover, you will not worry about wasting ink when you are trying for unusual shades. Put extra ink of reddish tone in one can, grays in a second can, and so on. As you add odd tones from various projects to these "bases" you will find weird and wonderful colors developing. At best you will achieve a deep glowing color, at worst your "base" will be a soft gray tone that you can use for mixing subtle off-colors.

*Seal cans of leftover ink
with a layer of oil or water*

Seal each can by pouring a small amount of boiled linseed oil onto the surface of the ink. The oil on top will form a skin, keeping the ink underneath moist for as long as a year. You can also use water in this way to form a temporary seal. If you do not seal your cans with oil or water, your block printing inks will soon become hard and dry out.

Many printers use a waxy, round "skin paper" pasted down firmly on the surface of the ink to keep the surface moist. They then pour their thin sealing layer on top of the wax paper. This is the best method to keep ink from drying out, but it is a bit inefficient for a block printer who is constantly dipping into one ink pot or another for smidgens of color to use in mixing various shades.

It is not necessary to have tops on the ink cans. Replacing the lid on the can does not keep the ink from drying out, and unless you wipe the rim carefully, the lid is likely to get stuck onto the can. I do not use lids on ink pots unless I am carrying them about for a demonstration. A metal tackle box with the extra tray removed makes a fine kit box in which to keep your ink cans.

CLEANING YOUR EQUIPMENT

When cleaning your block at the end of a printing session, wet it thoroughly with solvent, kerosene, or turpentine, and then wipe it dry with a soft, clean rag. A block with many fine lines should be gone over with a scrub brush. The bristles of the brush fit down into the lines and clean them most effectively.

The brayer should also be soaked with solvent, especially the ends near the metal core rod, and then wiped clean and dry and hung up on its nail. A gelatine brayer can be cleaned with turpentine, kerosene, or benzene, but not with water. Gelatine dissolves in water and will melt if exposed to concentrated heat. The surface of the roller is rather easily dented and should be protected with a jacket of oiled paper when not in use. A brayer is best stored in a cool dry place hanging from its handle.

Wipe your palette clean and dry.

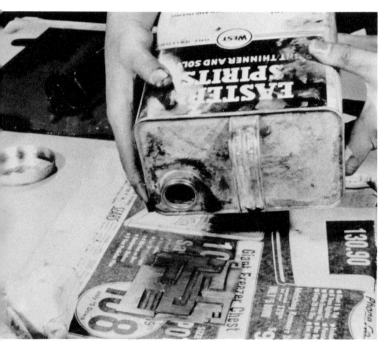

After printing, clean the block with solvent

Use of small scrub brush to clean out fine lines and crevices

Wipe it dry with a soft cloth

90

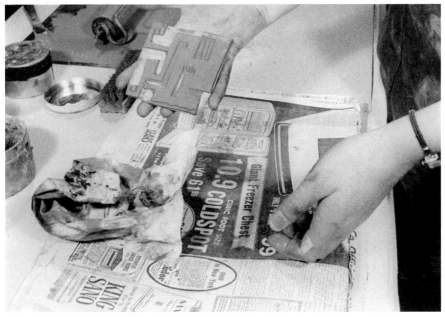

The clean block should look like this

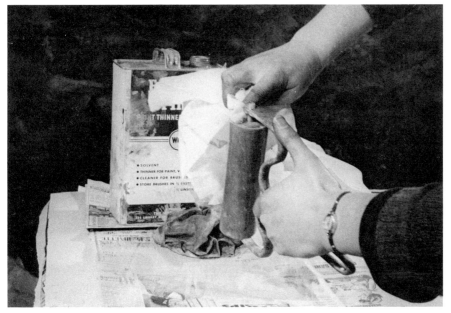

The brayer deserves a thorough cleaning

91

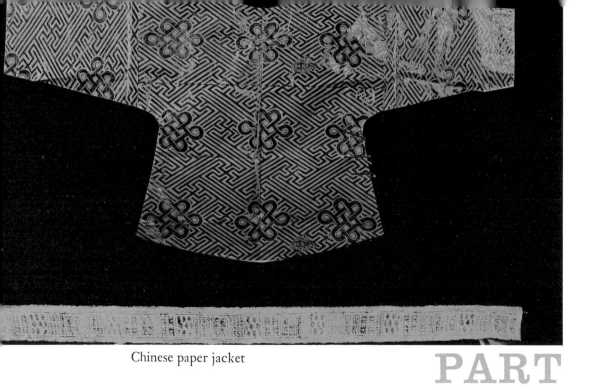

Chinese paper jacket

PART

Courtesy of The American Museum of Natural History

4 *Special Projects*

NOTE ON HOW TO USE THIS SECTION: This section contains general directions for various projects, elaborating techniques that you will need to use for each. You can apply many of these suggestions to other projects not specifically described.

DRAPERIES

A drapery design can be large or small, very simple or extremely complex, depending upon the effect you want to create in your room. A drapery fabric should not be monotonous to look at or overpowering in effect. It will be a part of the background of your life and must be pleasant to live with. The design must be as attractive draped as it is spread out flat because in use it will be gathered into folds.

Measuring your windows for draperies is simple. Decide first on the finished length you want from the top of the window frame to the bottom. Add six inches at the bottom for a double three-inch hem. The amount you add at the top for a heading will depend upon the kind of pleat you intend to make. A simple, gathered heading requires about a three-inch hem. For French pleats with buckram

Primitive art inspired this reverse-repeat design
utilizing a single block

94

"Four Seasons" To hang gracefully when
closed, a drapery should be full

*Simple, rectangular blocks create
a bold drapery design*

95

and hooks you usually need six inches. The new self-pleating tapes, used with four-pronged hoods, need only a one-inch heading.

The style of drapery you are planning will determine the number of widths of fabric you need to allow for each window. Simple side draperies for small windows have been made from a single length of thirty-six-inch wide fabric split down the middle. It is simpler to handle a piece like that on the bed, if you pull a thread to indicate where the fabric will be divided. You can then cut it after it has been printed. Draw draperies need quite a lot of fullness to hang gracefully when closed. The usual rule is to measure the width of your window, and then double this. For some very sheer fabrics you can triple the width to give a luxurious effect.

The width of your fabric and how many yards you have to print will help you to decide how large to make your block. Printing a three-inch square block all over several two and one-half-yard lengths of drapery fabric can be a discouraging job. If your design is small, cut several exact duplicates of your design motif and mount them on a big piece of cardboard to make a larger block.

I like to make my drapery blocks as large as possible. With four prints of a block eighteen inches long and fifteen inches wide I can print one yard of a thirty-six-inch wide fabric. It takes quite a while to cut such a large block, but the printing time saved is considerable.

When planning the size to make your block, you can allow for

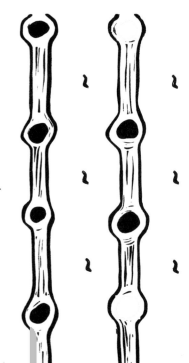

A large block saves printing time.
Opposite: *This cheerful design was inspired by a chemical formula. The colored circles (red, yellow, and blue) were printed separately —*
Freda Hall Lipmann

96

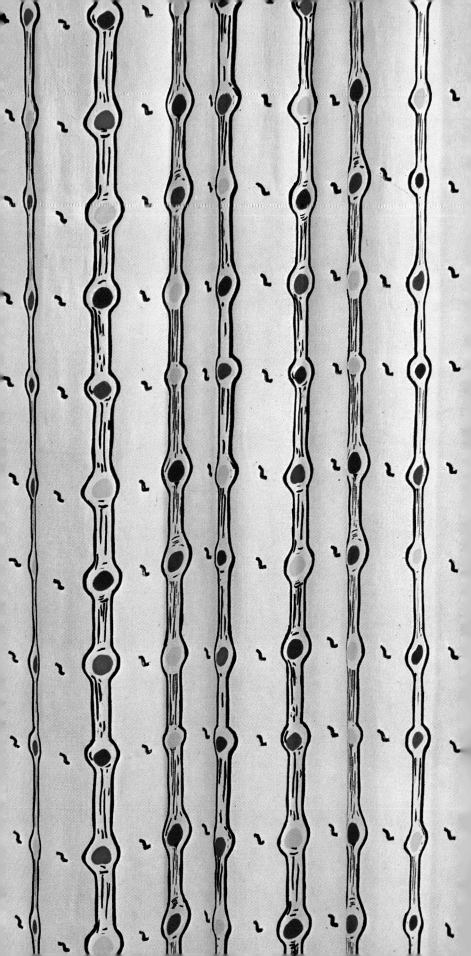

a one-inch to three-inch unprinted margin at either selvage. This plain edge gives a finished look to the printed length. Also, the fabric is easier to pin to shape, and the blocks are simpler to place accurately if you allow for this extra fabric.

Never make pencil or chalk marks on the fabric; they are too hard to wash out. Fasten a small safety pin at the places you want to mark, such as where the hem and the heading will be. Stretching a string across the fabric to show where the hem and heading will be turned up is sometimes helpful.

I like to leave a small unprinted margin at the top and bottom of each block printed length. This sets off the design and also emphasizes the point that the design has been made especially to fit this particular length of fabric and not cut from one of many six-hundred-yard bolts of machine printed fabric. Also, the margin gives you a good spot to print your personal signature block.

PLACEMATS

A placemat can be made in any size, from twelve by eighteen inches up to sixteen by twenty-four inches. Beyond this size it would be a tablecloth, and a mat smaller than twelve by eighteen inches would be called a napkin by most women. The dimensions you decide to use will be determined by such factors as the size of the table the mats will be used on, the diameter of the plates usually used on the table, and the width of the fabric you plan to print.

A forty-two-inch fabric could be cut into mats twelve by twenty-one inches. A thirty-six-inch fabric cuts economically into twelve by eighteen inch mats. A yard will make six mats. These mats would probably shrink to eleven by seventeen and one-half inches. Most shrinkage occurs along the warp, or the length of the goods.

Don't forget that the design on the placemat should not detract from the silver, glass, and china for which it makes a background. Plan your design full size and put a plate on the sketch to see if your arrangement of the motifs will balance with the center of the mat

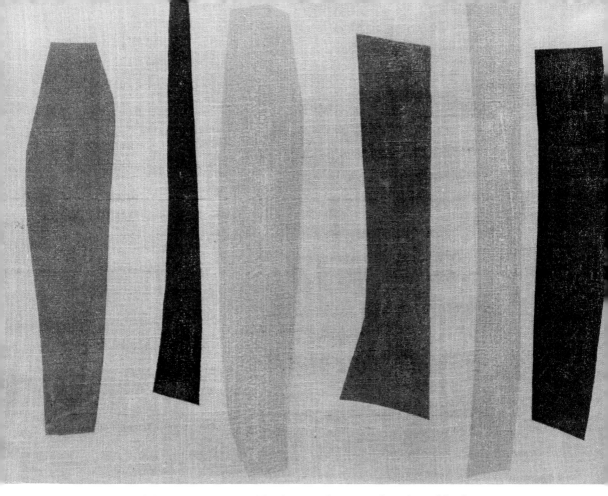

A bold design printed in three analogous colors from blocks of cardboard — Ellen Waring

covered. If you want to make napkins, will they be plain or printed, the same color as the mat or of a contrasting fabric?

Fabric for placemats should be printed as one length. When printing a set of placemats, do not chop your length of goods into many small pieces before printing. You will find it much easier to handle one long length of fabric on the printing bed rather than many small ones. Also, it is much simpler to stretch the length accurately, making it more likely that your mats will be printed identically, if you wish them to be.

Experiment freely with color to get decorative effects. Let your imagination take over. Try using a different color fabric for

100

each mat, keeping the design and print color the same. Or use the same color background but change the ink color for each print. Combinations are endless, but be careful to keep some of your elements the same so that the finished prints will harmonize.

You must plan now how you will finish the edges of your mats. They can be rolled by hand or made with a wider hem and machine stitched. A fringed edge is the easiest to make. Run a stitch along the base of the fringe to prevent further raveling. This is simple to do neatly if you have a zig-zag sewing machine; otherwise use a straight stitch.

If sewing does not appeal to you, try printing on ready-made placemats. They are available in beautiful, plain fabrics and intriguing colors. If you can use several dozen of a similar item, you can usually arrange to buy them wholesale. If you live in a fairly large city, look up wholesale dry goods merchants in the classified section of your telephone book. Country dwellers could write to the Chamber of Commerce of the nearest big city for information.

"Goose Girl" A linen tablecloth using three separate blocks —
M. Wallach, Handcraft Studio, Lime Rock, Connecticut

Non-repeat designs improvise a new pattern with each swirl of the skirt

SKIRTS

Consider accessories when planning prints to wear. When planning a skirt, a jacket or shorts, for example, consider what can be worn to complete the costume. Try to use at least one color in your design that can be easily matched in blouses and other accessories.

Non-repeat designs are especially well adapted to printing on skirts and shorts. You can concentrate the pattern at the hem line if you want, with some prints scattering up towards the waist. Or, if it is more flattering to you, you can arrange the stronger areas of print at the waistline. A strong border design printed around the bottom of a gathered or pleated skirt can be difficult to wear gracefully, especially if a matching blouse is not available. For a more attractive line, try carrying a bit of the border up toward the top of

102

the skirt. Bold designs block printed in strong colors are usually most effective made into garments of simple styling. More elaborate detailing in style and sewing is appropriate for quieter, all-over designs printed in subdued colors.

Choose a good basic skirt pattern in the style and size you want and cut the pieces accurately, marking each piece as you cut it. When fabric is wet it stretches, and it is sometimes hard to tell the right side from the wrong.

Gathered or straight pleated skirts, which can be made from a single piece of fabric printed lengthwise, are easiest to cut and sew. For a very full skirt, print three yards of thirty-six-inch wide fabric. You can cut the waistband from the extra length. Use less fabric for a pleated skirt, or if you prefer less fullness.

Fabrics with definite weave and napped fabrics must be cut carefully. When using a very wide fabric, or one with a definite weave such as shantung, or a nap like corduroy, cut two lengths, allowing for a hem and for shrinkage. Baste one seam, and this length can be spread on the bed and printed as a single piece.

A simple half-circle skirt is very flattering. When making this skirt, it is most practical to cut the skirt pieces out first. If you baste all seams except the back, the whole skirt can be stretched on the bed and printed at one time. The seams should only be basted, not machine-stitched, at this stage. If you have to print over a seam, you will find that the ink from the block cannot penetrate far enough into the seam to cover it completely. When the piece dries you will see an unprinted line at the seam. If you just baste the seam before printing, this unprinted area can be taken into the seam when it is machine stitched.

Full circle skirt pieces should not be basted together. Because a full circle skirt requires about four yards of thirty-six-inch wide fabric, it will hang more gracefully if cut into two pieces. These two pieces will be so large that it is usually easier to print them separately.

A full circle skirt can be printed with a straight block. The design will hang vertically front and back and horizontally at the sides.

*Large reverse blocks must
take into consideration
the circular form of the skirt*

104

The handsomest full circle skirts that I have ever seen are those planned especially for a circle. The pattern radiates from an imaginary point in the center of the waist. The block itself is a wedge shape. To plan a block like this, you should first make a large dummy from newspaper or wrapping paper exactly the same size as one quarter of your full circle skirt, minus the hem allowance and the seam allowance at the side. This dummy can now be folded in half, or in quarters, or in thirds, or into whatever segment of a circle you want. Choose a wedge shape that will be small enough to be manageable without limiting the scope of your design.

If the style you want is a complicated one, it is sometimes easiest to print a length of fabric and cut the skirt afterwards from this length. The waste scraps can be used for trimming other blouses and skirts.

Think about the waistband itself. Will it add to the design if printed or would it be better left plain? Also, the inside of the waistband is a good place to sign your hand-blocked skirt.

Your designs to wear can be zany or dignified, but remember that the object of any fashion is to enhance the charms of the wearer, not to bedazzle by itself.

NECKTIES

The necktie presents a rather special problem. A necktie of the conventional four-in-hand type is a tricky thing to sew, requiring a very nice and skillful hand, and a bow tie needs to be exactly detailed and painstakingly finished. Unless you are a clever seamstress, it is better not to get involved in these intricacies, since you can buy good-quality, ready-made washable neckties. Linen and silk ties print beautifully. Some silk ties are so fine that they take a good print when dry.

Before printing a ready-made tie, cut out a piece of light cardboard the exact shape of the front of the tie. Slip this between the lining and the front of the tie to make a smooth backing upon which to print. This will protect the lining and the back section of the tie

Designs inspired by nature and animals provide charming ideas for scarves — Stell and Shevis

from any ink that might penetrate through from the print, and it will eliminate the possibilities of "holidays" in the print from the lumps in the lining. The cardboard should fit snugly enough to keep the fabric of the tie taut and flat.

Lay the tie out on clean papers, and lightly sponge the section to be printed with clean water. Ink your block as usual, and then print the tie. Leave the cardboard in the tie while it dries, and you will not have to press it afterwards.

SCARVES

The shape of a scarf is quite variable. Often it is not a square but a triangle. Some women like ample thirty-six-inch squares that can be wrapped about their heads babushka fashion. Others prefer a more dainty eighteen-inch scarf, and some find a long narrow oblong, stole-like scarf most useful. Whatever the style, most women agree that the fabric must be fine, light, soft, and silk.

106

Marvelous as man-made fibers are, none has yet been machine-spun to match the lovely luminous qualities of real China silk. Because of its soft lightness, silk is difficult to print and requires delicacy in handling and designing. When pinning it on the bed, you should use common pins instead of T-pins to avoid holes in the fabric that can lead to "runs" in the silk. Also, the black ink from fresh newspapers will sometimes lift off the newspaper onto the back of a wet block printed in a light yellow or pastel color on a white silk. To prevent this, cover the thick newspaper bed with sheets of plain newsprint paper.

To make a successful print on silk, you must cover your block very carefully and very lightly with a fine, even coat of smoothly rolled-on ink. Use ink of the same consistency as for printing on heavier fabrics, but use much less of it, and roll it out much more. A heavily-inked block would make a stiff, unpleasant print.

Be especially careful not to add much linseed oil to the ink when printing on silk. Excess oil will cause the ink to spread and bleed along the fibers of the silk, resulting in a fuzzy print. This bleeding may not take place until several hours after the print has been made. If in doubt about an ink, make a test print and let it dry overnight.

When stepping on the block, be very careful that it does not slide on the smooth silk. Keep one foot solidly on the block to steady it, and press with the other.

When designing a block to be printed on silk, try to keep the pattern as linear as possible. Thin lines will not deposit as much ink on the scarf as heavy solid areas. It is best not to use a design that involves printing a solid area of one color over a solid area of another. Two solid layers of ink, no matter how thinly applied, will be stiff.

WALL HANGINGS

Wall hangings serve many purposes in contemporary architecture. They are very effective against the quiet, natural textures favored by modern architects for domestic interiors. And in our cities,

German wall hanging
Courtesy of the Metropolitan Museum of Art
Rogers Fund, 1909

109

steel and glass shells are being built that imaginatively conceived wall hangings could do much to humanize. In many public buildings where there are acoustical problems, wall hangings are being used to deaden the clatter of everyday noises. The Metropolitan Museum of Art has used wall hangings extensively as backgrounds for paintings. Many churches and synagogues are using especially-made wall hangings with decorative and symbolic designs that add to the atmosphere of worship as well as serving various practical purposes.

Wall hangings can be made with a variety of techniques. When designing a wall hanging, you do not necessarily have to worry about problems of repeating, or color matching, or draping. You can be imaginative and inventive. Different textures and techniques can be combined in a single hanging. Heavy wool rug yarn can be effective when used to accent a block printed design, or you can appliqué soft fabric spots on rough, heavy textured cloth. The block print in this background will change where the textures and colors of the fabrics change. Tie dye effects make interesting backgrounds for block prints too, and sometimes the accidental effects of the ties suggest design motifs you can carry further in the blocked overprints.

Be ingenious because a wall hanging can be anything you want to make it. It can be lined, or the edges can be hemmed or left raw and fringed. You can tack it up by the corners or sew a hem at the top and slip a pole through it.

MADE-UP GARMENTS

By exercising a little imagination you will be able to devise ways in which to spot-print small blocks on garments that have already been sewed together. Slip a very thick pad of newspapers under the single thickness of the fabric, where you are going to print, to make a bed for the block and also to protect the back of the garment from any ink that might penetrate through from the print.

Spot-printing can be very useful. Many paint and ink-splattered skirts and shirts have been saved for further wear by a strategically placed butterfly or flower print. A bright blossom print, or perhaps a simple, decoratively cut abstract shape, makes an attractive addition to a skirt or blouse and is certainly much more pleasing.

GREETING CARDS AND
HAND BLOCKED PAPERS

Designing a greeting card is a bit different from designing a fabric. The edge of your card forms a frame, and you must fill the area within this frame in a pleasing way. Simplicity is always a good rule. Decide what is most important and eliminate the things that do not add to this idea. And, since you are cutting a special block, you can make the motif and message as personal as you wish.

Lettering on the block must be carved in reverse

Historic holiday customs as well as the contemporary folkways of other peoples are rich sources of design inspiration for greeting cards. And you will find that a fresh approach to the much abused symbols of our holiday seasons can make a card with a not particularly original idea seem exciting and quite special.

When you are planning a card, it is more economical to look first for the envelope you will send it in. You can then work out the size of the card to fit nicely into your envelope and look for a paper that can be cut easily to that size. You can often buy odd lots of attractive envelopes from large stationery stores in packages of fifty or one hundred.

You can block print on most kinds of papers and light cardboards. The absorbent rice papers are made in Japan especially for block printing. They are available in many sizes, textures, colors, and at many prices. Most art stores carry a selection. Lithograph and

112

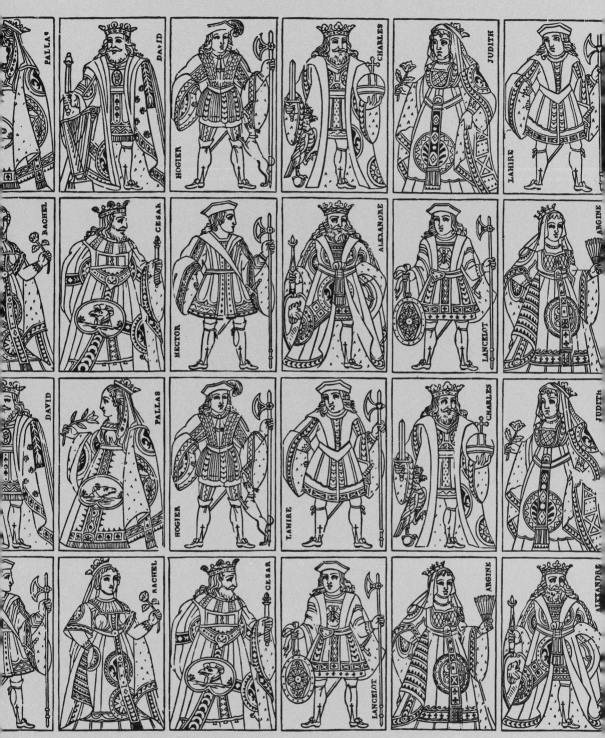

German 17th century playing cards
Courtesy Cooper Union

etching papers are handsome in texture and often absorbent enough to be excellent for block printing. A graphic arts supply house will have many different types in stock. Generally, the heavier papers are more expensive. Some heavy, textured papers, however, will not take ink except under great pressure. It is inadvisable to buy them unless you have a screw-type press.

Because of their great absorbency, non-woven fabrics made for filter papers and disposable dish-rags and the dressmakers' stiffening called "pellon" are excellent for multicolor block printing. You can overprint six or seven colors and not get that unpleasant shiny surface that means the fibers of the paper are too full of ink.

Look for unusual papers that will enhance the unique qualities of your design. One of the nicest Christmas cards I ever received was printed on a page from an old telephone book. Of course, very smooth shiny papers are not satisfactory to print on. Blocks slip on the shiny surface, which does not absorb the ink.

If you have bought paper in large sheets, try tearing it for an attractive edge. Use a heavy flat ruler on the paper for a guide line. If you prefer, a paper cutter will give you a clean edge, or you can cut through several lightweight sheets at one time with a sharp mat knife.

When it comes to folding your card, the conventional single fold is good if you are using a stiff paper or cardboard. For lighter paper a French fold is practical, or try an accordion fold, either lengthwise or sideways. If you want a really big card you might work out a variation on the road map fold. Consider, when making a folded card, the elements of your design and try to handle them so that one is led naturally from the beginning page to the end.

Some heavy papers print better when they are slightly damp. The easiest way to dampen paper is to put as many sheets as you are going to use between two wet blotters under a heavy drawing board or sheet of glass. The weight keeps the paper from wrinkling as it gets damp. Ten to twelve hours should be enough to dampen all of the sheets of paper.

*Christmas card printed in two colors
with registered blocks — Stell and Shevis*

*Christmas card printed with linoleum bird
and wood scraps — Stell and Shevis*

Very large cards can be printed on a bed on the floor. And if
your cards are to be cut from a full-size sheet of large paper, it is
often easier to print the blocks first and cut the paper afterwards.

Small blocks can be printed on a table top. Use a folded newspaper or a thick magazine for a printing pad and press the block by
leaning your full weight on it. If the pressure of your weight has not
made a good print, hit the back of the block once or twice with a
rubber mallet.

Gift paper printed in several colors

Calendar pages printed in two colors — Stell and Shevis

117

You can make very beautiful toned prints on rice paper by rubbing. Lay the inked block face up and carefully place a sheet of rice paper down on it. Starting from the center of the block, rub the back of the paper with a round smooth tool, such as the back of a wooden spoon. You can control very exactly the quality of your print. Rub very hard where you want solid dark areas and more lightly for grayer tones.

Prints on paper will dry much more quickly than those on cloth. Most prints will dry in twenty-four hours. If you are in a great hurry, get some special dryer from the company that makes the ink. Soft absorbent papers will dry more quickly than smooth shiny ones.

LETTERING

Block printers have a treasury of letter forms from which to choose. Scribes and, later, type designers have created for us a fascinating variety of beautiful, intriguing, expressive, and sometimes odd letter forms. A, B, C and the rest of the letters of the alphabet

118

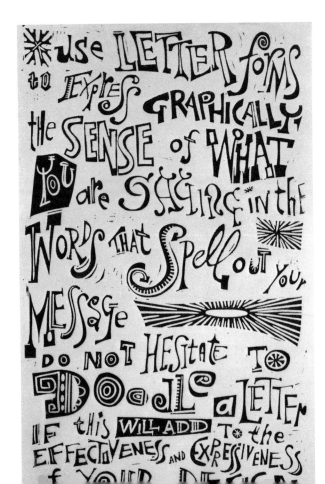

*Use LETTER forms to express GRAPHICALLY the SENSE of WHAT You are SAYING in the WORDS THAT Spell out your MESSAGE DO NOT HESITATE TO DOODLE a LETTER IF this WILL ADD TO the EFFECTIVENESS and EXPRESSIVENESS of YOUR DESIGN

*Single block of experimental letter forms
printed on linen (above) and paper (opposite)*

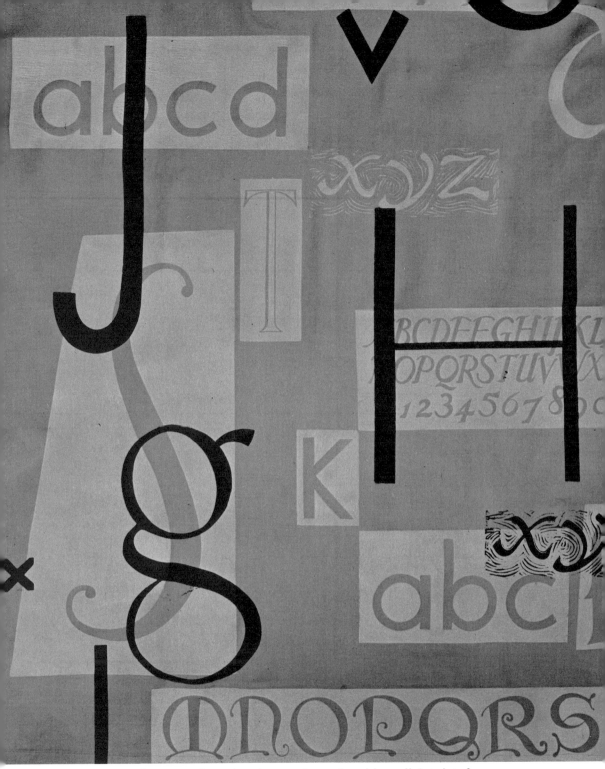

Letters and numbers in negative and positive relief, printed in overlapping patterns, make a handsome drapery

are often used in building block patterns for curtains in children's rooms. In addition, many people want to cut monogrammed blocks for spot-printing on ready-made garments or for bridge tablecloths and bedspreads, cocktail napkins and aprons. And, of course, you may use lettering in your greeting cards and sometimes in your hand-blocked papers.

Experiment with several ways of cutting letters until you find the method that is easiest for you. The design must be cut in the block in reverse, of course. Plan on tracing paper the lettering that you want to use. Turn the paper over, and the design will be reversed. You can use a piece of white carbon paper to transfer it to the linoleum, or rub the front of the tracing paper with chalk to make it a carbon, as described on page 34.

When designing greeting cards, it is sometimes fun to combine all the different letter styles of which you can think, in sizes from giant to minute, to express the joyous abandon of a special occasion. In the drapery called *Pi*, illustrated opposite, I have used the letter forms themselves as design motifs. Some of the letters are much larger than others, and the styles of letters are scrambled in a non-repeating arrangement. You can build an excellent and very stimulating lettering reference file by clipping from newspapers and magazines words and sentences lettered in various styles that appeal to you.

Use letter forms to express graphically the sense of what you are saying — the words that spell out your message. Do not hesitate to doodle a letter if this will add to the effectiveness and expressiveness of your design.

Egypto-Arabic lettering, 10th century
Courtesy of The Metropolitan Museum of Art
Gift of George D. Pratt, 1931

Block print by an eleven-year-old girl

5 Block Printing for Children

CHILDREN LOVE TO MAKE BLOCK PRINTS. They like cutting the blocks and mixing the colors, but particularly they have fun stamping on the block and enjoying the results. Designing presents few problems to the natural artists who are our children. Children revel in the infinite decorative possibilities of imaginatively manipulated blocks, brayers, colors, and textures. This freedom to improvise on fabric or paper can be an exciting classroom experience for both students and teacher. Of course, the teacher must know what she is doing technically and must take care to form good habits of craftsmanship in her students. Children should be given good equipment and shown how to use it and how to clean and care for it properly. Bad tools and poor materials result in shoddy work and much disappointment. The ink consistency must be correct, beds should be carefully made, and lots of kerosene available for cleaning.

In some situations it is not wise or possible to use special cutting tools. In this case vegetables, such as potatoes, carrots, parsnips, and turnips, can be cut with a paring knife into small blocks that children can print with regular block printing inks or with poster paints, if they are working on paper. These vegetable blocks will dry out and

Children can easily be taught to use block printing tools

124

Their own designs, easily executed, intrigue children

A beautiful design from the animal world is created by an imaginative child

shrink in a few hours. A similar block can be made from an art gum or a solid rubber eraser, which will last indefinitely.

Children can also make complicated designs in blocks of plasticene without sharp tools of any kind. One surface of the gob of plasticene should be smashed flat on a smooth surface. This side must be really flat to make a block that will print well. Then, designs can be poked in the flattened side with fingers or a pencil. Since the

Plasticene block prints have many uses, such as this gay placemat

block of plasticene is oily, it has an affinity for oil base printer's ink and can be used to make effective prints on fabric or paper. This kind of block should be printed by leaning on it at table top level. Too much weight would squash the block flat and obliterate the design. A plasticene block, treated rather gently, will last quite some time. When the child is through with it, it can be cleaned and smashed up to resume its place on the modeling table.

Small blocks can be inked with a pounce if a brayer is not available. Dip the pounce into the ink and rotate it to distribute ink all over the bottom. Dab the pounce carefully over the block until it it is completely covered. Be careful to avoid heavy gobs of ink on the block.

126

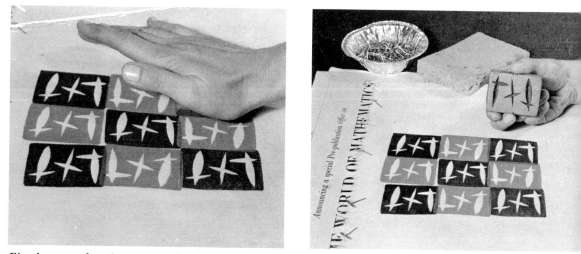

Firmly press, but do not squash, the plasticene for a print

To make a big block without gouges, children can use the rubber from old inner tubes. The tubes can be bought from auto junk yards for a few cents apiece. They can be cut with scissors in simple silhouette shapes. These shapes are then mounted, using rubber cement or Elmer's Glue-All, onto heavy cardboard. Excess cardboard background should be cut away to avoid grief from careless inking. Often several children working together with their individual blocks on a single piece of fabric or paper can produce striking results.

Designs made from inner tubes should not be planned too large because the rubber tube is formed on a circle. A small section, up to about five inches, can be flattened, but a bigger section would need to be rather cleverly cut out in a linear pattern to lie flat.

Large simple shapes cut from light wood with a jigsaw make very effective blocks because the grain of the wood adds its own intriguing texture to the print.

This sheet of practice prints was made with the vegetables pictured above

BLOCK PRINTING WITH VEGETABLES

*The delightful designs on this and the following page were
printed by artist Tomi Ungerer using potatoes, tomatoes,
onions, lemons, and carrots. They indicate the variety
of ideas available to children — everything from humorous
animals and birds to their own patterned wallpaper.*

Copyright 1961 by Tomi Ungerer

128

129

BLOCK PRINTING WITH INNER TUBES

*This print was made by a twelve-year-old student at St. Luke's
School in New York City. The original block above, with its figure
cut from the inner tube, was inked and printed three times
to achieve this lively effect.*

FIBER	FABRIC	TEXTURE	COLOR
LINEN	Belgian linen	medium	natural white and colo
LINEN	canvas	rough and somewhat stiff	natural and wh
LINEN	drapery linen	rough	natural white and colo
LINEN	crash	medium smooth	natural
SILK	crepe	very smooth and drapes well — has a dull surface	white and colo
SILK	taffeta	smooth and stiff	white and colo
SILK	satin	very smooth and shiny	brilliant — white and colo
SILK	chiffon	medium	white and colo
SILK	shantung	medium with slubs	natural white and colo
SILK	Japan silk	very smooth, soft, and shiny	white and colo
JUTE	burlap	very rough and prickly	natural and co some colors fa

WEIGHT	SHRINKAGE	NOTES	USES
medium and heavy	very little	prints very well	upholstery skirts table cloths table mats draperies couch covers
medium and heavy	very little	takes a bold print very well	draperies table mats wall hangings
heavy	varies but usually not much	prints very well	draperies upholstery table mats
heavy	about an inch to a yard	prints very well	table linens wall hangings
varies from light to heavy	varies — but this is a fabric with a lot of "give"	prints very well if handled carefully, usually should be printed dry	stoles scarves carefully-styled garments
varies from light to heavy	very little	print dry	elegant garments
varies from very light to very heavy	usually very little	prints very well	garments scarves heavier for drapes, upholstery, wall hangings
very light and semi-transparent	usually none but is very stretchy	stretch on the bed, dry and dampen to print	scarves garments
varies from light to medium	usually very little	prints very well	draperies garments scarves
very light	usually not much	prints very well if block is inked lightly	scarves blouses
medium and heavy	not much	prints best dry	draperies wall hangings table mats

FIBER	FABRIC	TEXTURE	COLOR
COTTON	velveteen	napped — very smooth and soft	white and col
COTTON	felt	smooth	white and col
COTTON	terry cloth	very rough	white and col
COTTON	jersey	very smooth	white and col
COTTON	theatrical gauze	rough open weave	white and col silver and gol
COTTON	monk's cloth	medium	natural and c
COTTON	one-ply monk's cloth	smooth	natural
COTTON	Indian head	medium	white and col
COTTON	hopsacking	medium smooth	natural
LINEN	handkerchief linen	very smooth	white and col
LINEN	Irish linen	smooth	white and col

134

WEIGHT	SHRINKAGE	NOTES	USES
varies from medium to heavy	varies, but usually not much	prints very well	draperies upholstery garments
medium to heavy	PRINT DRY DO NOT WASH		skirts wall hangings
light to heavy	very little	takes bold prints very well	beach wear towels, etc.
light to medium	usually not much — it is naturally stretchy	prints well	garments
very light and transparent	varies	print boldly so design will show on open weave	draperies wall hangings
very heavy	about 3 inches to a yard but also stretches in use	prints well	draperies couch covers
medium	very little	prints very well	draperies couch covers skirts
medium	very little	does not print well	
medium	very little	prints very well	light draperies
very light	very little	prints well but block must be lightly inked	handkerchiefs fine blouses napkins
medium	very little	prints very well, drapes well	skirts table mats and cloths napkins wall hangings

FIBER	FABRIC	TEXTURE	COLOR
COTTON	unbleached muslin	smooth	natural
COTTON	sheeting	smooth	white and colo:
COTTON	percale	very smooth	white and colo.
COTTON	broadcloth & pima cotton	very smooth	white and colo
COTTON	denim	smooth	colors
COTTON	osnaberg	rough and stiff	natural
COTTON	pebble cloth	rough drapes very well	natural, white, and colors
COTTON	bark cloth	smooth with slubs	natural, white, and colors
COTTON	Tuscan satin	very smooth	natural and co.
COTTON	corduroy	napped with ribs	white and colo

WEIGHT	SHRINKAGE	NOTES	USES
...ery light ...o heavy	about 3 inches to a yard	heavily sized, prints well after washing	draperies skirts wall hangings
...edium	varies	prints well	draperies garments
...edium	very little	prints well	draperies garments
...edium	none	prints well and drapes well	garments
...edium ...d heavy	varies — about 2 inches to a yard	prints well	draperies shorts skirts jackets
...eavy	about 3 inches to a yard	heavily sized, prints nicely after washing	draperies couch covers slip covers
...eavy	varies — about 1 inch to a yard	print large bold block for best results	draperies wall hangings
...edium	varies — about 1 inch to a yard	prints well	draperies couch covers wall hangings
...ry heavy	none	prints very well	draperies wall hangings upholstery slip covers
...ries from ...ry light ...heavy	varies, usually not much	prints well	garments draperies slip covers

HISTORIC TEXTILE PRINTS

German block print for ecclesiastical embroidery, 15th Century
Courtesy of The Metropolitan Museum of Art
Rogers Fund, 1909

Persian wall hanging, 19th Century
Courtesy of The Metropolitan Museum of Art
Gift of Jacques Martin, 1927

140

Japanese wood block scroll, 8th Century
Courtesy of The Metropolitan Museum of Art
Gift of Benjamin Strong, 1930

141

Fragment of a 19th Century English textile, William Morris, 1834-1896
Courtesy of The Metropolitan Museum of Art
The Theodore M. Davis Collection, Bequest of Theodore M. Davis, 1915

Printed hanging from India, 17th Century
Courtesy of The Metropolitan Museum of Art
Gift of Harry Wearne, 1928

Block prints from India, 19th Century
Courtesy of The Metropolitan Museum of Art
Rogers Fund, 1909

Egypto-Arabic textile print, 13th-16th Centuries (Mamluk Period)
Courtesy of The Metropolitan Museum of Art
Gift of V. Everit Macy, 1930

144

Japanese floral motives
Courtesy of The American Museum of Natural History

Egypto-Arabic stamped and gilded textile, 10th Century
Courtesy of The Metropolitan Museum of Art
Gift of George D. Pratt, 1931

146

"The Thrasher," 20th Century textile designed by Raoul Dufy
and executed by Bianchini, Ferier

Courtesy of The Metropolitan Museum of Art
Gift of Edward Moore, Jr., 1923

148

French textile designed by Paul Poiret, 20th Century
Courtesy of The Metropolitan Museum of Art
Gift of Edward Moore, Jr., 1923

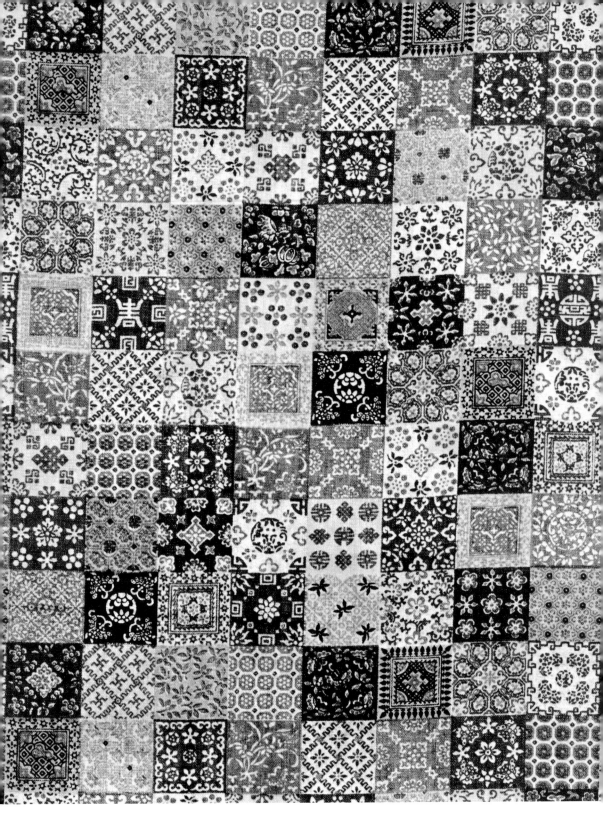

150

Chinese printed cotton, 19th Century
*Courtesy of The Metropolitan Museum of Art
Anonymous Gift, 1946*

Length for kimono, Japanese, 20th Century
Courtesy of The Cooper Union Museum

152

Resist print, American, 18th Century
Courtesy of The Cooper Union Museum

Russian textile, 17th Century
Courtesy of The Cooper Union Museum

154

Block print from Russia, 18th Century
Courtesy of The Cooper Union Museum

Direct print, "Gyotaku," by Yukoku Shimizu
Courtesy of The American Museum of Natural History

157

Printed textile designed by Raoul Dufy
and executed by Bianchini, Ferier, 20th Century
Courtesy of The Metropolitan Museum of Art
Gift of Mrs. Harry B. Wehle, 1940

Printed textile designed by Raoul Dufy
Collection Norman Kent

158

Chinese block-printed silk scarf
Courtesy of The American Museum of Natural History

160

Additional Fabric Notes

WOOL

There is a great variety of woolen cloths available. Wool can be printed successfully, but it is often frustrating to handle because it shrinks so much when wet. Also, wool fibers are very absorbent. They continue to drink up ink long after the print feels surface dry. After several months the print may have faded noticeably. Eventually it may even disappear completely, having been absorbed into the fibers of the wool.

Gaberdine is a twill weave that is used with many fibers, most usually a mixture of wool and a synthetic, but it can also be used with cotton. It drapes very nicely, and so is suitable for garments, but it does not have much dimensional stability, that is, it tends to sag. It is not such a happy choice for draperies or upholstery.

SYNTHETICS

Rayon, nylon, orlon, dynel and all the other test-tube fabrics can usually be block printed successfully. When in doubt, test a small swatch of the fabric you have in mind. Most of the traditional types of weaves are available in synthetic fibers or in mixtures of synthetic and natural fibers. *Butcher linen* is a mixture of cotton and rayon. There are many serviceable cotton and orlon or wool and orlon mixtures. *Nylon satin* is very strong. *Nylon chiffon* is filmy yet stiff, sometimes an advantage. Sometimes a synthetic fiber will take a print better when dry than it will when wet. *Fiberglass* should be printed carefully because it is quite slippery. It tends to sag and droop in spots when made into draperies. It is especially important to test your ink if you are going to print on a synthetic fabric. Some orlon and nylon blends do not take oil-base ink very well.

SPECIAL ACKNOWLEDGMENT

The ingenuity and delight in discovery shown by the individuals in my classes has always been a spur to my own imagination. Together we have worked out many of the techniques outlined in this book. Paul Coombs, my partner in Blockhouse of Boston, was instrumental in developing other procedures. To him and to the members of the block printing classes at the YWCA in Boston, at the Willimantic summer arts and crafts workshop, and to my always lively art students at the State University Teachers College at Buffalo, my thanks.

I am also grateful to my friends Stell and Shevis and to many former students for allowing me to use examples of their work to illustrate points in the text. I am especially pleased that the handsome block printed fabrics of Freda Hall Lipmann are so well represented.

EDITOR'S NOTE: Unless otherwise acknowledged, all work reproduced in this book is by the author.

PHOTOGRAPHIC CREDITS

(*all others noted in captions*)

FERDINAND BOSCH	
28	85 (right)
29	94
71	106
73 (bottom)	107 (bottom)
79 (top)	120

WALTER FLEISCHER				
26	53	59	81	95 (left)
31	54	60	83	111
41	56	75 (left)	89	112
48	57	76	90	126
52	58	80	91	127

INDEX